BITCOIN

TRADING

FOR BEGINNERS

The complete guide on how to Make Insane Money Investing and Trading in Bitcoin

BY Smith, Luk Brandon

BITCOIN

INTRODUCTION: 9

CHAPTER 1 11

ALL ABOUT BITCOIN BUSINESS 11
THE BITCOIN MARKET 12
THE PROCESS OF PURCHASING BITCOINS..13
VALUE OF CRYPTOCURRENCY OR VALUE OF BITCOIN 14
THE STOCK OF BITCOIN IS ANTICIPATED TO INCREMENT RADICALLY.........14
BITCOIN MERITS ESTEEM AS A METHOD FOR THE STORE OF SIGNIFICANT
VALUE AND TRADE OF CASH 14
THE UNSTABLE IDEA OF BITCOIN WILL GET WIPED OUT 15
WIDESPREAD ACCEPTANCE OF BITCOIN IS REQUIRED 15
ADVANTAGES FROM BITCOIN ADVERTISING ARE PLENTY 16
MAKING THINGS POSSIBLE FOR BITCOIN ADVERTISING AGENCIES 17
WHAT ARE THE KINDS OF BITCOIN EXCHANGES?...........................18
P2P PLATFORMS 18
DEALERS 19
CFD PLATFORM 19
BENEFITS OFFERED BY A BITCOIN ART GALLERY 20
BRINGING IN MONEY TRADING BITCOIN WITH THE LATEST BITCOIN NEWS
TODAY 22
SERIOUS BITCOIN TRADING WITH THE HELP OF INFORMATION AND NEWS.22
HOW TO START YOUR OWN BITCOIN EXCHANGE - TIPS TO SECURE YOUR
EXCHANGE? 23
BITCOIN AND BINARY OPTIONS TRADING 25
HOW TO BUY BITCOINS? 27
HOW TO PARTICIPATE IN THE BITCOIN ECONOMY...........................32

CHAPTER 2 36

BITCOIN MINING 36
SHORT HISTORY OF BITCOIN 36
WORKING OF A BITCOIN: 39
BECOME A MAJOR PART OF THE MARKET:......................................39
BITCOIN MINING 40

ABOUT BITCOIN AND BITCOIN TRADING 43
BITCOIN MINING STEP-BY-STEP GUIDE FOR BEGINNERS 44
GET A BITCOIN MINING EQUIPMENT 44
HOW THE BITCOIN MINING GAME HAS CHANGED? 51
IS BITCOIN A SECURE INVESTMENT FOR THE FUTURE?.......................55

CONCLUSION: **65**

TRADING

INTRODUCTION 69

CHAPTER 1: VALUE INVESTING 72

THE THREE PRINCIPLES OF VALUE INVESTING 74
HOW TO GET STARTED 75
FOREIGN INVESTMENTS: WHY SHOULD TAKE THE LEAP 77
THE KEEN METHOD TO MAKE UNFAMILIAR INVESTMENTS 78
VANGUARD TOTAL INTERNATIONAL STOCK ETF (VXUS) 78
ISHARES MSCI PACIFIC EX-JAPAN (EPP) 79
VANGUARD EUROPEAN STOCK INDEX FUND (VEURX) 79
UNDERSTANDING YOUR MIND WILL MAKE YOU A BETTER INVESTOR 79
MY FAILED INVESTMENT 80
CONCEPT ONE: YOUR TWO MINDS 80
HOW SHOULD THIS INFLUENCE YOUR INVESTMENT CHOICES? 81
CONCEPT TWO: PRIMING 82
CONCEPT THREE: SNAP DECISIONS AND MISREPRESENTATION 83
WARREN BUFFET: THE ULTIMATE VALUE INVESTOR 84
WORTH INVESTING TOOLS 85
TOP ASSET MANAGEMENT TOOLS 90
WHAT'S THE MESSAGE? 92
STRATEGY 2: GROWTH INVESTING 93
DOES GROWTH INVESTING WORK? 94
WHAT IS GROWTH INVESTING? 95
STEP 1: PREPARE YOUR FINANCES. 97
STEP 2: GET COMFORTABLE WITH GROWTH APPROACHES. 97
STEP 3: STOCK SELECTION 99
BUYING GROWTH FUNDS 100
SCREENING FOR GROWTH STOCKS 101
STEP 4: MAXIMIZE RETURNS. 102
INVESTING IN HOT SECTORS 103
UNDERSTANDING EARNINGS 104
GROWTH INVESTING THROUGH VALUE INVESTING 104
USING THE PRICE-TO-EARNINGS RATIO 105
POPULAR TYPES OF GROWTH INVESTMENTS 110

MAKES A GOOD GROWTH STOCK 114

CHAPTER 2: MOMENTUM INVESTING 117

THE FATHER OF MOMENTUM INVESTING 117
PRECEPTS OF MOMENTUM INVESTING 118
ELEMENTS OF MOMENTUM INVESTING 118
MOMENTUM SECURITY SELECTION 119
TIGHT RISK CONTROL 119
PERFECT ENTRY TIMING 121
POSITION MANAGEMENT 121
PROFITABLE EXITS 121
ADVANTAGES OF MOMENTUM INVESTING 122
DISADVANTAGES OF MOMENTUM INVESTING 123
DOES IT WORK? 124
THE APPEAL OF MOMENTUM INVESTING 125
SHORTING 125
STRATEGY 4: DOLLAR-COST AVERAGING 126
A WISE CHOICE 127
ONCE YOU'VE IDENTIFIED YOUR STRATEGY 128
GET STARTED INVESTING AS EARLY AS POSSIBLE 131
DECIDE HOW MUCH TO INVEST 132
OPEN AN INVESTMENT ACCOUNT 132
UNDERSTAND YOUR INVESTMENT OPTIONS 134

CHAPTER 3: DAY TRADING PSYCHOLOGY 136

7.1 UNDERSTANDING TRADING PSYCHOLOGY 136
7.2 TECHNICAL ANALYSIS 138
7.3 DAY TRADING TERMINOLOGIES 138

FAQ'S ABOUT DAY TRADING 144

CONCLUSION 148

Introduction:

Bitcoin made in January 2009 as advanced currency by a strange individual named Satoshi Nakamoto. It is utilized for online installment components under a decentralized position. Bitcoin has no actual appearance, yet every one of the exchanges done is confirmed by a monstrous measure of registering power. It isn't accessible in any bank or government and not important as product or value, but rather it generally on high in the rundown of cryptographic forms of money and triggers the dispatch of significant virtual financial standards. You can do trading this digital money and make high advantages or benefits on your venture.

Bitcoin trading is likewise something very similar to purchase the Bitcoin at low and sell at an exorbitant cost. The value of it decides by people who participate in it. However, you need to comprehend the unpredictability of Bitcoin trading. As a lot of brokers and specialists accept that Bitcoin value graphs are incredibly helpful for trading, a considerable lot of them also accept that these are the basic tool for Bitcoin value investigation today.

Also, these can be utilized for trading the advanced money expertly likewise with them trading choices are made dependent on certain realities and investigation. Despite what at the reason Bitcoin's cost live apparatus can be very valuable as it will control you through the trading.

So, every one of the people who have exchanged values knows well that it is so essential to way specialized outlines. Also, in Bitcoin trading, there ought to be some value diagrams that show where the costs are going.

A lot of brokers accept that when you are trading advanced money, it is significant for you that you way the most recent Bitcoin news yet, in addition, the value development. With Bitcoin value investigation today you can make beneficial trading and in any event, when you are trading the cryptographic money scantily, you should search for Bitcoin value outline.

Bitcoin has worldwide allure and a lot of globalists accept that this is the currency for the future. Moreover, a ton of Bitcoin organizations will put resources into the possibility of the cryptographic forms of money. The enormous objective crowd can be covered at no time with Bitcoin promotion. This prompts more odds of cooperating with people keen on a promoted business.

Hence, you can browse numerous techniques as per your inclinations and objectives; in any case, you need to comprehend that whichever strategy you will utilize, should contact your focused on crowd.

Chapter 1

Bitcoin is known as the absolute previously decentralized advanced cash, they're fundamentally coins that can send through the Internet. 2009 was the year where bitcoin was conceived. The maker's name is obscure, in any case, the false name Satoshi Nakamoto was given to this person. Bitcoin exchanges are made straightforwardly from one person to another through the internet. There's no requirement for a bank or clearinghouse to go about as the center man.

Because of that, the exchange charges are an excessive lot of lower, they can be utilized in every one of the nations throughout the planet. Consistently more traders are beginning to acknowledge them. You can buy anything you need with them. It's feasible to trade dollars, euros, or different financial standards for bitcoin. You can buy and sell figuratively speaking some other nation money.

These wallets are situated on your pc, cell phone, or on outsider sites. Sending bitcoins is straightforward. It's just about as basic as sending an email. You can buy anything with bitcoins. The justification for this is that bitcoins are not attached to any country. They're not dependent upon any kind of guideline. Independent ventures love them since they're no MasterCard expenses included. They're people who buy bitcoins only with the end goal of speculation, anticipating that they should raise their value.

Bitcoin set up a different method of advancement. The days' truth is that bitcoin is changing the world's accounts like how the internet fundamentally altered distributing. The idea is splendid. Exchange charge decreases are a reality of bitcoin. Tolerating bitcoins cost anything, likewise, they're exceptionally simple to set up. Chargebacks don't exist. The bitcoin local area will produce extra companies, so.

Bitcoin is the digital cash that is utilized to buy a variety of labor and products everywhere in the world. Bitcoin likewise exists in actual structure however it's accessible in advanced, the essential structure implied for internet exchanging by utilizing wallet programming or some other online assistance. Bitcoins can be acquired through mining or by exchanging different types of cash or even a few labor and products.

The Bitcoin Market

The Bitcoin market is a very wide market. There are specific kinds of exchanges for which Bitcoins are the solitary type of payment that is generally acknowledged. Assuming you need to gain that particular great, Bitcoins will be needed to finish the exchange.

When you venture into the Bitcoin market, the primary thing you need to learn is the way to secure Bitcoins. The primary alternative is to buy them. It will require little effort to do it so. The subsequent choice is to mine them. Mining happens on programming that plays out certain numerical conditions for which the merchant has compensated some Bitcoins. This is serious time taking and numerous brokers say that it bears a little segment of natural product.

· You should connect your wallet to your financial balance to allow the buyer to start.

· You will require wallet programming in request to turn into a part of the Bitcoin market. You can likewise get online assistance all things being equal. There are online wallet administrations accessible in every significant country so you won't confront any difficulty in setting up your wallet account.

· Once your financial balance is connected, you will see a buy Bitcoins interface in the product window. This will be basic.

The Bitcoin market deals with the very systems that are utilized in some other kind of exchanging market. When the cost of Bitcoins turns out to below, it's a sign to get them. When the cost turns out to be high, you can offer them to acquire a benefit. Mining can be hard, yet all brokers should in any case attempt it every once in a while. It is somewhat lethargic thus you should show restraint. You will require Bitcoin mining programming. There are in any event, mining pools. You need to just decode a square with the joint effort of a mining bunch. You will then get Bitcoins as indicated by your commitment.

Remember, the value of Bitcoins goes all over in no time. If you don't take the perfect action at the perfect time, you can lose a huge segment of your speculation. Something to be thankful for is that once you completely comprehend the essentials, you can harvest bunches of benefits from this type of exchange.

Value of Cryptocurrency or Value of Bitcoin

Bitcoin is an astounding philosophy of executing cash regardless of the boundary over the internet. It is under the authority of a decentralized organization having a reasonable arrangement of rules and guidelines. Thus, a superb and effective substitute for halfway controlled bank cash. It has tremendous inescapable fame.

The stock of Bitcoin is anticipated to increment radically

It is expected that the Bitcoin supply will stretch around 21 million in the coming years. The current stockpile of Bitcoin is practically 13.25 million. In like clockwork, there is a reduction in the rate at which Bitcoin is delivered by practically half. The inventory of this crypto coin is expected to cross 19 million and surprisingly more in the following four years (by 2022).

Bitcoin merits esteem as a method for the store of significant value and trade of cash

Bitcoin merits its privilege as a significant perspective both as a method for capacity and a method of trading cash. It will not be right to specify that the capacity of Bitcoin as a store of significant value relies upon the capacity as the foundation of cash trade. When you use at some point as a store of significant value, it needs to have a natural value. If Bitcoin has no accomplishment as a cash trade stage, it will likewise have no allure as a store of significant value.

Bitcoin is viewed as unstable, and this is one of the excellent worries that regularly debilitate its acknowledgment and reception in the financial framework. In any case, as an ever-increasing number of people and undertakings are putting resources into this crypto coin and getting related with the digital currency, it is accepted that soon the unpredictable nature will show a diminishing.

Besides, it is likewise accepted that it will acquire authenticity in most of the countries and there will be a specified structure in the financial framework for the cryptographic money to work one next to the other with the conventional financial forms.

If you give a nearby glance at the current market value of this crypto coin, you will find that it is exceptionally affected by speculative premium. It by one way or another presentation the highlights of a Bubble, which has sensational cost increment and high media consideration, particularly in the years, 2013 and 2014, it is accepted that as the money accomplish its acknowledgment and reception boundless in the standard financial economy, the theoretical viewpoint in Bitcoin will diminish.

Various nations are available to digital money. These are the nations that have played intensely in the extension too. Various Bitcoin trades are working from these nations and give profoundly shifting levels of wellbeing, security, protection, and power over your assets and data.

So, the interest for better items goes up, generally. Bitcoin trades are playing out their obligation well; however, it is your due constancy to pick the one that you can trust. Likewise, you should pick a wallet where you will keep your Bitcoin before choosing a trade. The greater part of the trades is offering types of assistance in major worldwide financial forms like USD, Yen, Euro, and so forth.

Advantages from Bitcoin Advertising Are Plenty

For example, if there is some organization that necessities compelling publicizing that can arrive at the majority, Bitcoin promoting is the best thing. Truth be told, large-scale manufacturing needs mass-selling, and publicizing makes this conceivable. Through publicizing, the organization can spur interest for its item and keep up it consistently.

In this way, it is tied in with discovering the arrangement and contacting wide crowds. Besides, Bitcoin promoting also ensures the organization against unreasonable rivalry because people in general figure out how to perceive the brand and the name of the maker. It also arrives at the portion that can be focused on explicitly.

Bitcoin publicizing likewise making tension on the retailer to stock the products which have a decent interest, as else, he would risk losing his user to his rivals. More people are opening their brains to the presence and dependability of such stages and searching for more prominent freedoms.

Numerous people are longing to split away from according to the administering bodies engaged with the capacity and trade of their resources. Indeed, the future may appear to be faint this day however as more innovative personalities cooperate to make more advantageous in the manner money and everything financial is dealt with and to grow it further Bitcoin publicizing is required.

Exchanging Platforms

Consider a business deal that is coordinated through a specialist that brings the buyer and the seller together. Generally speaking, there is a little commission that the go-between takes from both the get-togethers. A comparative thought is followed by the trading stages, who go probably as the specialists between the buyers and merchants of the diverse digital types of cash. The customers at the two completions of the trade never need to meet each other, and the portion is driven through a shielded entry that is joined by the exchange.

P2P Platforms

This is one more technique for purchasing progressed assets, and after some time, the thought has ended up being unmistakable as well. There could be no specialist in this kind of trade. The P2P organizes simply partner the buyers, and the vendors to each other, and the expense of the benefits are settled and counseled by the two social events included.

The P2P platforms offer a lot of companies, for instance, a protected method for the portion between the two get-togethers, and there is a little organization charge for that. There is an extended peril in this kind of trade since you don't have even the remotest clue about the person that you are coordinating business with.

Dealers

Similar to the trading stages, the trader objections empower the customers to buy Bitcoins and altcoins. In any case, as opposed to partnering the buyers with the merchants, the exchange goes probably as the buyer similarly as the seller.

Generally speaking, the expense of the mechanized assets is higher when appeared differently about the trading stages, yet the system is way simpler. Unquestionably the most by and large pervasive facilitating exchanges join Coin Mama and CoinBase.

CFD Platform

Short for Contract for Difference, these are without a doubt the most un-secure exchanges out there. The fundamental standard drew in with the trades on these exchanges is that you, as a customer, bet on the expense of Bitcoin and distinctive altcoins. You don't have any modernized asset, yet you bet on the expense as a trade-off for the fiat financial structures that are offered in the spread.

These stages moreover outfit you with a decision to utilize your bets by getting cash from the exchange. While it may sound extraordinary on paper, it includes a lot of peril, and youngsters and fledglings should keep an essential separation from these exchanges.

If you have never at any point considered looking at a bitcoin craftsmanship display, you should realize that you have been passing up some lovely significant benefits that would permit you to see exchanging merchandise from an alternate perspective. When you have a piece of art that you might want to sell utilizing customary methods, you hazard managing some lovely unsavory circumstances. However, if you somehow managed to sell or buy craftsmanship with bitcoin, the circumstance would be extraordinary.

As a matter of first importance, you should realize that as long as you utilize the administrations gave by a bitcoin craftsmanship display, you don't need to stress over your protection. Perhaps the most intriguing advantage related to bitcoin exchanges is that they are mysterious, which implies that nobody can follow your specialty exchange back to you.

So, if you have been clutching a family painting for quite a while frame currently, however, have arrived at a point where you simply need to sell it with no family members deciding for you, choosing a bitcoin art display is the correct approach.

Presently, another fundamental benefit that you will profit from when you buy craftsmanship with bitcoin is the way that you don't need to hang tight for a long time before your exchange is settled. Getting back to the fundamental point, exchanging art, this particular benefit can truly change how you buy or sell your fine arts. It would be suggested that you search for a group of experts that has different stockrooms and display areas all through the world.

Another significant benefit related to the choice to buy art with bitcoin is the way that you don't need to stress over paying high exchange charges. Because of the way that this money is an advanced one that has nothing to do with outsiders - banks, governments, or some other financial foundation, the value of the bitcoin stays as before. You don't need to stress over swelling or anything identified with it. Indeed, you can be sure that exchange expenses are kept to a base when exchanging utilizing bitcoin.

This way, you will experience no difficulty in putting away and displaying your bits of craftsmanship in the one that is found closest to you. The best part about depending on the correct experts is the way that they can store and show you are fine art in a similar spot, accordingly saving you a lot of cash simultaneously. Simultaneously, you won't need to stress over your work of art being taken care of twice as much when you need it displayed in an exhibition where potential buyers can see it.

Merchants who are earnest realize well that exchanging can be beneficial when they approach the most recent Bitcoin news. When you start with the rudiments truly, in the blink of an eye you will wind up being an expert dealer in the market acquiring bigger value than the contributed one. Entryways like Live BTC News can be of extraordinary assistance for such brokers and financial backers.

So, you don't lose anything with getting the hang of, teaching yourself in the field of BITCOIN, as keeping yourself refreshed brings information as well. It is also simple to explore starting with one page then onto the next on these sites if you are among numerous people who consistently needed to think about BTC however had no clue from where to learn.

Serious Bitcoin Trading with the Help of Information and News

There are alternate methods of learning Bitcoin exchanging, such as perusing financial magazines, exchange news which at last covers the news identified with the BTC market. Bitcoin news today depends on realities and estimations rather than experience and genuine issues. The experts realize where precisely is the highlight take the data and use it for better. Each exchanging choice dependent on the data and the most recent Bitcoin news will in general make benefits for brokers and financial backers.

With cybercriminals focusing on crypto trade stages, online protection is the highest need of bitcoin trades. This has driven numerous reliable trade stages to put resources into new and progressed safety efforts to offer improved assurance to their users' assets.

If you are hoping to put resources into a trade and are considering how to begin your bitcoin trade, acquire understanding into the accompanying tips to assemble a safe trade.

Time-locks

An inventive answer for secure bitcoin exchanges, particularly at the hour of withdrawal, is to utilize time-bolts that require two keys and a specific period to finish a bitcoin exchange. If the subsequent key isn't utilized to affirm the exchange, the exchange is switched, making it practically unimaginable for programmers to pull out reserves.

Two-factor verification

To improve the security of people exchanging accounts, most trades utilize two-factor verification (2FA) when their users sign into their exchange accounts. Two-factor verification requires users (at the hour of joining to their records) to give their user name and secret word, alongside an affirmation code that is imparted to them either using an instant message or a mechanized voice call. Regardless of whether somebody takes a user's login subtleties, the person in question would be not able to get to a user's record since the affirmation code would in any case be needed to sign in.

Multisig

While grasping how to begin your bitcoin trade, see how multisig can work for your advantage. Multisig, short for multi-signature, requires more than one private key to approve a bitcoin exchange. Many significant trades embrace this innovation to get their users' wallets and give an additional layer of safety.

Cold storage

Cold storage can likewise be utilized to give an additional layer of safety while shielding users' assets. Cold storage alludes to the disconnected storage of bitcoins in a chilly wallet. It is helpful for the people who exchange bitcoins value a huge sum. As the coins are not put away on the internet, it turns out to be almost outlandish for programmers to get to users' assets.

KYC check

Some bitcoin users like to exchange on trades that don't need KYC checks because these users need to exchange secretly. However, truly bitcoin trades that require character checks offer a safer stage to users for exchanging. If each person associated with exchanging passes a trade's KYC confirmation measure, the danger of extortion is incredibly diminished as people who enjoyed ill-conceived exchanging can be effortlessly perceived.

Protection approaches

Another path for a trade to upgrade its security is by buying a protection strategy that covers digital assault and any misfortune from specialized breakdowns. For instance, nearby trades in Japan can buy committed bitcoin trade protection that covers misfortunes due to operational issues, digital robbery, and theft by representatives. With the expansion in bitcoin exchanging volumes and trades taking care of more exchanges day by day, network safety has gotten basic. Many significant trades are receiving trend-setting innovations to upgrade their security and give their users a stage that permits secure, quick, and continuous exchanging.

While you look for counsel on the most proficient method to make your bitcoin trade, try to zero in on these tips to fabricate an exceptionally secure trade stage. This will help assemble likely financial backers' advantage in your trade. Also, accentuate making your foundation easy to use so it is not difficult to comprehend by your intended interest group.

Bitcoin and Binary Options Trading

Twofold alternatives have been getting an ever-increasing number of well-known over the most recent 2 years. This kind of exchange has been wanted among new dealers as they don't have to buy anything, simply foresee whether the resource will go up or down in a predetermined period. Those exchanges are going on in brief periods (30 secs, 1 min, 5 min) however maybe months as well. If the broker anticipated wrongly, they will lose their cash. If the merchant was directly in his/her forecast, they will get an 80-85% payout, contingent upon the representative.

Paired choices are here and there alluded to as 'win big or bust choices', 'advanced choices', or 'fixed return choices (FROs), which are exchanged on the American Stock Exchange. Bitcoin (BTC) is digital money that is made and held electronically and nobody controls it. "Bitcoin is an online payment framework imagined by Satoshi Nakamoto, who distributed his creation in 2008 and delivered it as open-source programming in 2009.

The framework is distributed; users can execute straightforwardly without requiring a middle person. Exchanges are confirmed by network hubs and recorded in a public circulated record called the blockchain. The record utilizes its unit of record, also called bitcoin. The framework works without a focal archive or single chairman, which has driven the US Treasury to order it as decentralized virtual money. Bitcoin is frequently called the principal digital currency... "

Bitcoin as a money in paired alternatives exchanging

Bitcoin is currently a generally utilized money and many exchanging stages acknowledge it as a technique for payment for their customers' exchanging stores. There are numerous advantages of utilizing Bitcoin as money. The main advantage is "the way that the expense of exchange is the most minimal among all types of online payment. This is the very motivation behind why Bitcoin was made in any case, to bring down the expense of the online exchanges. Since there is no focal authority overseeing Bitcoin, no assistance charge is paid when getting or communicating payment."

How to Buy Bitcoins?

As bitcoin is fresh out of the box new money that has as of late approach, numerous people are not mindful of what it is and how it very well may be helpful. It is like the US Dollar, Peso, and even Euro yet the lone distinction is that a solitary government or a solitary organization can't handle it. Bitcoin is a decentralized distributed cash. It is associated with the PC of each person working with it.

Thus, it is digital money and there is no requirement for a national bank for performing exchanges utilizing this cash. It has now become a hot item among the observers. The exchanges utilizing advanced financial standards happen immediately and there is no exchange charge included. Best of all, no one can control the bitcoin network.

Assuming you are keen on advanced financial forms, you should realize how to buy bitcoins as well. A few groups say that it is truly hard to manage bitcoins however actually getting bitcoins is extremely simple. If you need to realize how to buy bitcoins, you should begin figuring out how to utilize wallet programming. Then, you should figure out how to send and get cash so you can buy bitcoins. Most importantly, you will require a wallet.

You should have one on your PC excessively to comprehend bitcoins because some exploratory trades will be included. If you need to protect your cash, it is ideal to continue moving it by trading coins.

The most well-known strategy for purchasing bitcoins is to get them from trade. There are a lot of sites accessible today that work with the acquisition of advanced financial forms. These trades don't sell the bitcoins themselves. They pair a buyer with a bitcoin vendor. These trades request that the user give some close-to-home data before the trade can happen.

Another approach to gain bitcoins is to mine them. Each bitcoin that exists today was once mined through the Bitcoin Mining Network. However, mining can be incredibly unsafe. Its trouble increments with time and it turns out to be practically unimaginable for a user to acquire benefits.

That is not everything; you can buy digital money from a private representative as well. You can go into a trade with the merchant to get bitcoins however this accompanies a few disadvantages. The trade will be mysterious. You don't have any idea about any genuine insights regarding the agent except his wallet number however you need to move assets to get the trade going. Bitcoins can assist you with bringing in cash and for this, you simply need to realize the opportune chance to make the trade.

The world has concurred that a Bitcoin gives a put-away proportion of significant value similarly that gold and silver have all through the ages. Like gold and silver, Bitcoin is just value that the other person will pay you for it. This has prompted cheating since exchanging started.

The Bitcoin dream has been to police its local area and stay past the actual examination of any worldwide government. The Utopian dream was wrecked before a month when Mt. Gox, shot the biggest Bitcoin trade, shut down because of security penetration and burglary of around $300 million value of Bitcoin. Users who had Bitcoin on the store with Mt. Gox don't have the foggiest idea of the amount they'll get back.

The issues at Mt. Gox expose the network safety contention. Shockingly, Bitcoin as money has shown wonderful versatility. This versatility could be only the lift expected to legitimize the money and the lean towards the legislative association that may help this juvenile store of significant value take off to its standard potential.

The circumstance of the Mt. Gox episode may end up being an aid for the cash. By far most of the business cash exchanging is done through trade arrangements which is the reason we follow the business dealers in our own exchanging.

A trade arrangement is fundamentally a protection strategy that gives ensured esteem at a particular point on schedule to secure against money vacillations. It's what the product trades are established on. The trade markets are the interstates of the financial business. They measure monstrous volumes while gathering a little cost for every exchange. Thusly, the expense of the person trade is little yet the sheer volume of trades prepared makes it a tremendous income hotspot for the entirety of the significant banks.

The market's reaction ended up being organized. While costs fell no matter how you look at it, the market appeared to comprehend that it was a personal organization's concern and was subsequently limited to Mt. Gox users' capacity to get their cash out. Therefore, Bitcoin costs have settled at around $585. This is wealthy the December high of $1,200 yet close to the normal cost throughout the previous a half year.

The last circumstantially planned piece of the primary change from Bitcoin as a revolutionary, elective store of significant value that exists outside the standardized financial industry to be included into that equivalent financial framework is its capacity to be burdened by the physical governments it was created to evade.

The IRS has announced Bitcoin as property instead of money and is thusly dependent upon property laws as opposed to cash laws. It also wipes out contentions with the U.S. Depository and Congress over lawful delicate issues. It's just esteemed as a decent that can be traded for different labor and products, deal.

Bitcoin is a worldwide commercial center executing exchanges on an electronic organization. That sounds like a dreadful parcel like the forex markets. Private users of Bitcoin will fuss for the public authority to shield its kin from abnormal trades similarly as ranchers were cheated in the grain exchange of old Egypt or gold and steers by assayers and stockyards in the Wild West.

Tera Group might be in the perfect spot at the perfect time with the correct thought as Bitcoin may have demonstrated itself to act naturally supporting at the retail level. Institutional and lawful designs are being set up to proceed with its advancement as the financial business is left to find out some way to adapt it.

Bitcoin has based on the thought that cash is an item or any kind of record, acknowledged as payment for labor and products and reimbursement of obligations in a given country or financial gathering. Bitcoin utilizes cryptography, or numerical conditions, to control the creation and move of cash, as opposed to depending on governments and focal financial specialists.

Moves for credits, deals, buys, or some other strategies for payment can be prepared by anyone, utilizing a work area, cell phone, tablet, or PC. This is all conceivable without the requirement for a financial organization to go about as a delegate or recording specialist.

The Bitcoin economy is expanding at a fast rate, as an ever-increasing number of new companies enter the circle and attempt to offer conventional administrations however utilizing Bitcoins. As Bitcoin goes more standard, these are simply going to increment in number and extension, accordingly introducing a brilliant chance to jump aboard with this at a beginning phase.

The enormous benefit of entering the Bitcoin economy currently is that you'll get in on this innovation at the 'pioneer stage' and you'll have the chance to be one of the pioneers. Companies that work in the current Bitcoin economy also appreciate free exposure of their business inside the Bitcoin people group. Everything from the gift that acknowledges Bitcoins to buy store gift vouchers to EVR bar that got famous in the profoundly cutthroat bar and parlor scene in New York by tolerating Bitcoin as payment cash for drinks.

The benefits of being important for the Bitcoin people group should likewise be self-evident - in a real sense zero exchange expenses for trans-mainland cash moves, moment move of cash with no outsider postponements, and the capacity to arrive at everybody in the world who approaches the internet. The miniature Bitcoin economy is as of now prospering.

Presently you can do the conventional miniature assignments from offices like CrowdFlower on the Bitcoin stage and acquire your first Bitcoins that way. In case you're a business, there are a lot of good freedoms to publicize your business to the Bitcoin crowd through administrations like Coin URL.

On a person accounting front, it is ideal to keep a safe wallet online at one of the believed wallet administrations and afterward begin procuring some modest quantities of Bitcoin just to discover how this economy capacity and how you can use this. If you approach both fiat and Bitcoin in a fluid market, there are a lot of chances where you can pay in one and get in the other to take advantage of your business. The market is as yet not awesome and there are exchange opportunities through trades and labor and products.

Being essential for the Bitcoin economy at this energizing stage should demonstrate exceptionally advantageous to your business also. You'll have the option to contact a group of people that would some way or another be difficult to charm - people at the innovative front line of our general public.

How Halving Affects, the Bitcoin

The dividing produces results when the quantity of 'Bitcoins' granted to diggers after their fruitful production of the new square is sliced down the middle. Subsequently, this wonder will cut the granted 'Bitcoins' from 25 coins to 12.5. It's anything but another thing, nonetheless, it has an enduring impact and it isn't yet known whether it is positive or negative for 'Bitcoin'.

People, who are inexperienced with 'Bitcoin', for the most part, inquire as to for what reason does Halving happens if the impacts can't be anticipated. The appropriate response is basic; it is pre-setup. To counter the issue of money cheapening, 'Bitcoin' mining was planned so that a sum of 21 million coins could at any point be given, which is accomplished by slicing the award given to diggers down the middle at regular intervals.

So, it is a fundamental component of 'Bitcoin's presence and not a choice. Recognizing the event of the dividing is a certain something, however, assessing the 'repercussion' is a completely extraordinary thing. People, who know about the financial hypothesis, will realize that either supply of 'Bitcoin' will lessen as excavators shut down activities or The inventory limitation will move the cost up, which will make the proceeded with Operations productive.

There is no focal account framework in 'Bitcoin', as it is based on a circulated record framework. This undertaking is appointed to the excavators, thus, for the framework to proceed as arranged, there must be expansion among them. Having a couple of 'Diggers' will lead to centralization, which may bring about various dangers, including the probability of the 51 % assault.

Even though it would not naturally happen if a 'Digger' deals with 51% of the issuance, yet, it could occur if such a circumstance emerges. It implies that whoever will control 51% can either abuse the records or take the entirety of the 'Bitcoin'. In any case, it should be gotten that if the splitting occurs without a particular expansion in cost and we draw near to 51 percent circumstance, trust in 'Bitcoin' would get influenced.

It doesn't imply that the value of 'Bitcoin', i.e., its pace of trade against different financial forms, should twofold inside 24 hours when splitting happens. At any rate incomplete improvement in 'BTC'/USD, this year is down to buying fully expecting the occasion. So, a portion of the increment in cost is as of now evaluated. Also, the impacts are required to be fanned out. These include a little loss of creation and some underlying improvement in cost, with the track clear at a maintainable expansion in cost throughout some period.

This is actually what occurred in 2012 after the last dividing. However, the component of a hazard perseveres here Because 'Bitcoin' was in a better place than when contrasted with where it is presently. 'Bitcoin'/USD was around $12.50 in 2012 just before the splitting Occurred, and it was simpler to mine coins. The power and figuring power Required was generally little, which implies it was hard to arrive at 51% control as there were practically zero obstructions to section for the diggers and the Dropouts could be in a split second supplanted.

Unexpectedly, with 'Bitcoin'/USD at more than $670 now and no chance of mining from home any longer, it may occur, yet as indicated by a couple of estimations, it would be an expense restrictive endeavor. So, there may be a "troublemaker" who might Initiate an assault out of inspirations other than financial addition.

In this way, it is right to say that the real impacts of "the Halving" are likely great for current holders of 'Bitcoin' and the whole local area, which takes us back to the way that 'Satoshi Nakamoto', who planned the code that started 'Bitcoin', was savvier than any of us as we peer into what's to come.

Chapter 2

Short History of Bitcoin

Bitcoin is the head digital currency of the world. It is a shared currency and exchange system dependent on a decentralized agreement-based public record called blockchain that records all exchanges. It was the idealistic dream of cryptographers and streamlined commerce backers to have borderless, decentralized money dependent on the blockchain.

Their fantasy is presently a reality with the developing notoriety of bitcoin and other altcoins throughout the planet. Presently the digital money was first conveyed over the agreement-based blockchain in 2009 and that every year it was exchanged for the absolute first time. In July 2010, the cost of bitcoin was only 8 pennies and the number of diggers and hubs was very less contrasted with many thousands in number at present.

Inside the space of one year, the new elective currency had ascended to $1 and it was turning into a fascinating possibility for what's to come. Mining was generally simple and people were taking in substantial income making exchanges and surprisingly paying with it now and again. Inside a half year, the currency had multiplied again to $2.

While the cost of bitcoin isn't steady at a specific value point, it has been showing this example of crazy development for quite a while. In July 2011 at a certain point, the coin went crazy and the record-high $31 value point was accomplished yet the market before long understood that it was exaggerated contrasted with the increases made on the ground and it resurrected it back to $2.

December 2012 saw a sound increment to $13 however soon enough, the cost planned to detonate. Inside four months till April 2013, the cost had expanded to an incredible $266. It adjusted itself later on back to $100 yet this galactic expansion in value rose its fame for the absolute first time and people began bantering about a real genuine situation with Bitcoin.

2013 was the advancement year for the currency. Huge companies started to freely support the acknowledgment of bitcoin and blockchain turned into a famous subject for Computer Science programs. Numerous people at that point imagined that bitcoin had filled its need and now it would settle down. Yet, the currency turned out to be significantly more famous, with bitcoin ATMs being set up around the world and different contenders began utilizing their muscles on various points of the market. Ethereum fostered the first programmable blockchain and Litecoin and Ripple began themselves as less expensive and quicker options to bitcoin.

The mysterious figure of $1000 was first penetrated in January 2017 and from that point forward it has expanded multiple times as of now till September. It is a striking accomplishment for a coin that was just valued 8 pennies only seven years back. Bitcoin even endures a hard fork on August 1, 2017, and has risen almost 70% from that point forward while even the fork bitcoin currency has figured out how to post some achievement. Every last bit of it is because of the allure of the coin and heavenly blockchain innovation behind it.

While conventional financial specialists contend that it is an air pocket and the entire crypto world would implode, it is simply not realistic. There is no such air pocket since it has, indeed, consumed the portions of the fiat monetary standards and currency exchange companies. What's to come is very brilliant for bitcoin and it is never past the point where it is possible to put resources into it, both for the present moment and long haul.

Working of a Bitcoin:

When you purchase a Bitcoin, you trade your actual currency and get the advanced money in the type of a Bitcoin. It is extremely simple if you need to trade money you need to pay for it to get that currency. The same is the situation with Bitcoins. You pay the current pace of Bitcoin.

Essentially it's a sort of product. The majority of the trades working in the market rake in some serious currency by moving the money on the lookout. Indeed, as it appears simple to bring in currency by changing over the Bitcoins into Dollars, these trades lose their currency effectively as well.

Become a major part of the Market:

There are a few different ways of turning out to be major parts of the Bitcoin market. The least difficult path is to purchase a devoted PC and introduce some Bitcoins mining programming and begin decoding the squares. This interaction is supposed to be the most effortless way yet it's sluggish.

If you need to bring in currency quicker, you need to shape a group. You ought to sort out a Bitcoin pool containing four to five people. At that point, you can frame a mining pool and can unscramble the squares quicker than a person can do. The fastest method to bring in currency through Bitcoins is that you should go directly to the business sectors. Go for the trustworthy and dependable Bitcoins trades working on the lookout.

You most importantly need to enlist yourself. Join and make a record and afterward, you should react to the affirmations in like manner. This will stay up with the latest pretty much every one of the functioning loads of Bitcoins. A few companies have even begun tolerating installments in bitcoins.

Bitcoin Mining

The appealing cryptographic money and the various contemplations that harvest up in the personalities of the spectators regularly encompass not many clear inquiries - how can it appear and what might be said about its course? The appropriate response, in any case, is clear. Bitcoins must be mined, to make digital money exist in the Bitcoin market.

For Bitcoins, there's an elective method to hold the fundamental records of the exchange history of the whole flow, and this is overseen in a decentralized way. The record that works with the interaction is known as the "blockchain". The quintessence of this record may require huge loads of newsprint for showing up routinely at all mainstream Bitcoin news. Blockchain extends each moment, existing on the machines associated with the tremendous Bitcoin company. People may scrutinize the legitimacy, even genuineness, of these exchanges and their accounts into Blockchain.

This also is anyway supported, through the cycle of Bitcoin mining. Mining empowers the production of new Bitcoin and accumulating exchanges to the record. Mining involves tackling complex numerical computations, and the diggers utilize massive figuring ability to address it. The person or 'pool' that tackles the riddle, puts the ensuing square, and wins an award as well. Furthermore, how mining can abstain from twofold spending? Pretty much like clockwork, extraordinary exchanges are mined into a square. In this way, any irregularity or wrongness is precluded.

For Bitcoins, mining isn't talked about from a customary perspective of the term. Bitcoins are mined by using cryptography. A hash work named "twofold SHA-256" is utilized. However, how troublesome is it to mine Bitcoins? This can be another inquiry.

This relies a great deal upon the exertion and processing power being utilized in mining. Another factor of value referencing is the product convention. For each 2016 square, the trouble involved in mining Bitcoins is changed without anyone else basically to keep up the convention. Thus, the speed of square age is kept reliable.

A Bitcoin trouble outline is an ideal measure to exhibit the mining trouble over the long haul. The trouble level changes itself to go up or down in a simply relative way, contingent upon the computational force, regardless of whether it's being fueled or taken off. As the quantity of diggers rises, the level of benefits merited by the members reduces, everybody winds up with more modest cuts of the benefits.

Having singular economies and networks, digital currencies like Dogecoin, Namecoin, or Peercoin, are called Altcoins. These are options in contrast to Bitcoin. Practically like Bitcoins, these 'cousins' do have an immense fan-following and fans who are quick to bring a profound dive into the colossal sea and start to mine it.

Calculations used for Altcoin mining are either SHA-256 or Scrypt. A few other imaginative calculations exist as well. Simplicity, moderateness, and effortlessness can deliver it achievable to mine Altcoins on a PC or by utilizing uncommon mining programming. Altcoins are a clamped down 'to earth' contrasted with Bitcoins, yet changing them into truckloads of money is somewhat troublesome. Cryptographic money buffs can simply trust if some of them could observer the same galactic notoriety.

Bitcoin combination into people's lives is the most desired thing at present. Bitcoin devotees can have a lot of decisions when they are hoping to procure this advanced money. A Bitcoin trade empowers purchasers to purchase or sell Bitcoins by utilizing fiat monetary forms.

An ongoing, just as a secure exchanging stage, is offered by the trades. Excproductent and a constant craze consistently go with Bitcoins. With various fans who are quick to exchange Bitcoins, the youthful currency and all the furor encompassing it appears to grow somewhat consistently.

All the information related to it is by all accounts as significant as the actual currency. The meaning of a "Bitcoin wiki", an independent venture, can't be denied by any stretch of the imagination. It will go about as a storage facility of information for Bitcoin fans from one side of the planet to the other.

Bitcoin is a cryptographic money that was made in 2009 by an obscure person utilizing the pseudonym Satoshi Nakamoto. While the currency has been around for quite a while frame, its ubiquity rose a couple of years' prior when vendors began tolerating it as a type of installment. As well as utilizing it in your exchanges, you can likewise exchange it accordingly making gigantic benefits.

The advantages of exchanging the currency

There are a lot of reasons why you ought to think about purchasing currency. A portion of these reasons include:

Every minute of every day exchanging: Unlike the financial exchange that works during business hours, Bitcoin exchanging happens the whole day and night. The exchanging impediments are just on you late.

Worldwide: You can exchange currency from any piece of the world. This implies that a person in China can purchase or offer Bitcoin to a person in Africa or some other spot. This makes the currency critical as it isn't influenced by the economy of a solitary country.

The simplicity of section: Unlike the securities exchange and other exchanging channels, there are no boundaries to passage into the Bitcoin market. You should simply distinguish a vendor that you can purchase from.

It's unstable: Just like different monetary standards in the unfamiliar trade market, Bitcoin is profoundly unpredictable. This implies that it rapidly changes its cost because of slight

43

changes in the economy. If you exploit the changes, you can make colossal benefits.

Bitcoin Mining Step-By-Step Guide for Beginners

Bitcoin diggers are people liable for the confirmation and valediction of every exchange before it is added to a square to make a blockchain. When a digger puts the following square on the blockchain, he/she can guarantee a prize which is for the most part in the type of bitcoins. The more numerical estimations you settle, the more the prize.

Get a Bitcoin Mining Equipment
Bitcoin Mining Equipment

The mining scene is getting increasingly more intricate as higher calculation power is utilized in mining. Bitcoin mining is extremely aggressive and you need to do a satisfactory examination before putting resources into equipment. Before it was feasible to utilize your CPU to mine Bitcoins yet with the intricacy in mining, this technique is not, at this point practical. You need to purchase an exceptionally constructed PC whose principal reason for existing is bitcoin mining.

Secure a Bitcoin Wallet

Bitcoin Wallet

You need to have a wallet that is either neighborhood or online based to store your advanced currency. If your wallet is self-facilitated, you need a duplicate of the wallat.dat record to keep you from losing your speculation. One can even get wallets for their cell phone. The strongly suggested wallet is oneself facilitated or privately made wallet.

Discover a Pool to Join

Mining Pool

It is suggested that you decided to mine performance or join a mining pool. A mining pool is a gathering of excavators who meet up to share assets and offer prizes. A pool promises you quicker returns as you join your figuring power for more noteworthy outcomes. Each pool has its principles, reward strategy, and expense charged for mining.

Get a Mining Software for your Computer

Mining Pool

There are different free mining programs. If you are in a pool, it is fitting to counsel them while interfacing your pool to your program. The projects run in an order line and may require a clump document to begin appropriately.

Mine

It is vital to watch the temperatures carefully. A few projects like SpeedFan can hold the temperature under control. You would prefer not to change in a real sense exploding your venture before you even beginning working. Sooner or later, you should check the amount you are making to check whether your venture merits running on.

The Bitcoin Market

The Bitcoin money market can be unstable and has effectively experienced numerous highs and lows. The Securities and Exchange Commission has been watching out for Bitcoin and gave an admonition in May of 2014 that expressed the accompanying: "the ascent of Bitcoin and other virtual and advanced monetary forms makes new worries for financial backers. Another product, innovation, or development - like Bitcoin - can give rise both to fakes and high-hazard venture openings."

Numerous financial backers caution against putting resources into Bitcoins as it has extraordinary unpredictability and isn't viewed as a utilitarian currency. Since it has no characteristic value, Bitcoin is anything but a suitable venture vehicle for most. For example, a PC programmer can take the entirety of the Bitcoin currency from a proprietor. Furthermore, because of the value hazard, many cautions that the interest in Bitcoins ought to possibly be in limited quantities assuming any, so a huge swing in esteem will not antagonistically influence somebody's work.

An assortment of online retailers is starting to acknowledge Bitcoin as a satisfactory type of installment. Tesla.com is only one such business. In bigger urban communities, some property management companies are also tolerating Bitcoin as a type of lease installment for inhabitants with the benefit being that the money can't ricochet as a check can.

Purchasing Real Estate with Bitcoin

Home dealers are starting to consider extra approaches to showcase their homes and break new ground with regards to promoting. By posting a permanent place to stay for Bitcoin, vendors might have the option to profit from the media publicity and grow their potential customer base by permitting Bitcoin purchasers to enter the blend. In 2014, a couple of Bitcoin exchanges occurred and, maybe the most outstanding was home close to Lake Tahoe that sold for 2,749 Bitcoins. This compares to $1.6 million of genuine U.S. currency.

Companies are starting to arise that have some expertise in Bitcoins and land. One such company is Homes4Bitcoin. This site takes into account mortgage holders and specialists to list a property for Bitcoins. BitPremier is another site that represents considerable authority in Bitcoins. While it's not yet achievable for escrow, title, protection or local charge to be paid in Bitcoins, it might only one day be.

BitPay is a company that was set up to permit exchanges using bitcoin to handily happen. Like the PayPal idea, this company exclusively works around the bitcoin currency and has an allocated period for an exchange to be finished before the conversion scale must be recalculated since the Bitcoin swapping scale is continually fluctuating.

Do Bitcoin Miners Need Product Managers?

Have you found out about bitcoins? It's the craziest thing - people are currently composing their product improvement definition and imagining pristine currency! This money has no connections to any administration or country. The entire thing "lives" in the personalities of the PCs who together make up the Internet.

The math behind it is a smidgen complex, however, it is by all accounts filling in prominence and, all the more critically, you can purchase things utilizing bitcoins. Microsoft as of late declared that they would acknowledge bitcoin in installment for their products. How might the entirety of this affect product administrators?

To Play in The World of Bitcoins, You've Got to Become a Miner

So here's how bitcoins work. Initially, there were no bitcoins. At that point people beginning running a PC program ("mining"). This program tackled a mathematical question. When they tackled the issue, they would be compensated for their "mining" exercises with bitcoins from a focal area. The mathematical question at that point got more enthusiastically to settle and everybody returned to work. As bitcoins began to appear to an ever-increasing extent, people began to acknowledge them in return for genuine products.

When others saw that this was going on, they become inspired to accomplish mining. To tackle the mathematical question speedier, greater, quicker PCs were required. Interests in server farm assets were made and what had been something that people were doing at home on spare PCs immediately become a modern activity practically overnight. There was one wrinkle in this entire "print your currency" conspire.

Likewise, with "genuine world" monetary forms like the dollar, euro, yen, ruble, and so on the swapping scale for bitcoins is certifiably not something fixed. That implies on some random day, the value of the bitcoins that you own can go either up or down. If your business is associated with mining, any huge plunge in the value of bitcoins could to a great extent affect the productivity of your business.

ASCI or application-explicit incorporated circuit machines have shown up in the Bitcoin mining market. The primary machine showed up at an excavator's home in late January and since the time reports have been streaming in of dispatched ASCI machines discovering their way into digger's Bitcoin mining rigs. Since ASCI machines are planned explicitly for the undertaking of mining Bitcoin, they are profoundly compelling machines at what they are intended to do. Top-of-the-line ASCI machines have every subsequent hash pace of more than 1 million. A regular CPU running Bitcoin mining programming has every subsequent hash pace of 1.5.

The shipment of ASCI machines has been a distinct advantage in the Bitcoin world. Computer chips are not, at this point even upheld by Bitcoin mining programming. This pattern favors those keen on mining who also end up having a huge number of dollars lying around to be utilized on costly equipment, just as the early adopters of Bitcoin mining who probably have made a weighty benefit from their initial mining endeavors.

Those early benefits could be folded into the best-in-class equipment and apparatus arrangement to keep creating Bitcoins well into what's to come. Those excavators who are running generally incredible GPUs are being hit the most exceedingly awful by the ASCI advancement. The trouble is effectively mining a square of Bitcoin has expanded to a level that may cause the expense of power to exceed the payout a GPU digger will see in Bitcoin from one year to another.

The entirety of this theory is tied intensely to the soundness of the cost of Bitcoin going ahead. If Bitcoin stays around the current 30 USD level, the development will keep on advancing. ASCI to a limited extent has added to the assembly that Bitcoin has seen in the course of the most recent 2 months.

The USD swapping scale for Bitcoin has taken off from 10 USD to 30 USD. It is elusive a venture with that sort of return anyplace in the world, so it is normal for Bitcoin to attract consideration in late days. Yet, will this consideration last? What's more, if so will it bring more examination and unpredictability than steadiness on the youthful advanced money? In the drawn-out relative security is the one characteristic that Bitcoin should build up if it is to achieve the first objective of being feasible and cutthroat currency on a world scale.

So will Bitcoin rise above the current name of a theoretical instrument? The appropriate response lies in a tangled snare of factors that incorporate the expansive range of mankind: legislative issues, brain science, money, dread, opportunity, protection, security... and so forth Notwithstanding the result, it makes certain to be a captivating show.

Instructions to Stay in Business in The World of Bitcoins

As product administrators, if we need to have something to put on our product chief resume at that point, we must ensure that the company is a triumph regardless of what product or administration we are selling. On account of a bitcoin digger, we're selling a mining administration that makes esteem essentially by making more bitcoins. Something that we need to stay mindful of is the value of bitcoins because as the value goes down, the assets that we need to work with will be restricted.

When the mathematical question is settled, the company will have gotten more bitcoins for our work. The test is that PCs are turning out to be quicker and quicker and that is permitting more contenders to enter this market. As product chiefs, we need to find ways to ensure that the company can help our ability and increment registering assets. At this moment the universe of bitcoins is similar to agitated boondocks.

The standards have not yet been composed; notwithstanding, there is a lot of currency to be procured. Product supervisors have a significant task to carry out in staying with them that they work for above water by watching what's new with bitcoin trade rates and ensuring that the bitcoin mining limit is being boosted.

How All of This Affects You?

Product directors who are searching for a genuine test are the ones who will wind up working for a company that is occupied with mining bitcoins. There could be no other firm or product administrator expected set of responsibilities that we can take a gander at as a source of perspective when we end up in the present circumstance.

This is a genuine test. The company works a progression of PCs that invest their energy taking care of a numerical question that, once tackled, will give the company the assets that we need to continue onward. As product administrators, we need to stay mindful of what the current swapping scale for bitcoins is.

Furthermore, we need to consistently be searching for ways that we can extend the processing limit that the company uses to make bitcoins. This is a packed market and it might turn out to be more packed after some time as more players enter the market. With a solid controlling hand, a product chief can assist their company with continuing to push ahead in a steadily evolving market. If you are searching for a genuine experience, this may be the work that you need!

Bitcoin is online advanced money, very much like a dollar or a pound however with a couple of special cases. Presented by Satoshi Nakamoto in 2009, Bitcoin takes part in a distributed installment system where no go-betweens exist and products can be safely moved between any two people in the world. It is related to a weighty company of PCs and the unit of currency for the Bitcoin system (suitably called Bitcoin) can be essentially gained by joining the immense company.

Bitcoin gives a quick modest and secure exchange elective however few will leap over it. So the 1,000,000-dollar question waits, is Bitcoin safe speculation? Bitcoin is a couple of years old, an intriguing creation that has awed numerous and for the record has achieved a name in the top monetary outlines.

Its prominence has traversed and it has driven a portion of the top companies like Virgin Galactic to think about it as a value wellspring of installment. Bitcoin costs increment at paces of up to 10% and keep on overwhelming as the alpha of the market and this has made many keen on putting resources into it.

Its worldwide money and its creation and presence lie behind a complex and nerdy numerical calculation that empowers it to shadow government-related disasters. Examples of political precariousness and government idiocies that dive the economy down to disgrace and lead long periods of interests in money down the channel don't happen in the digital currency system. This makes a protected and cordial speculation opportunity with low swelling chances.

The Downside

With a consistently astounding potential gain, digital currency likewise has its downs. As referenced, this thing is as yet making infant strides; and with that comes incredible vulnerabilities. Bitcoin costs are unpredictable; as of now expanding forcefully and can vacillate at 30% to 40% in a month.

The world is as yet amazed at its development and there exist not many Bitcoin holders and Bitcoin. This prompts unanswered inquiries and cold dread among people as putting resources into another unusual 'gold mine' can yield obliterating impacts. Its freshness delivers an absence of guidelines and drives away expected financial backers.

The puzzle encompassing the Bitcoin system is the main consideration to be thought of. Anything can occur and everybody taking an interest in the Bitcoin market is on a high ready. China in December 2013 dispensed with the utilization of Bitcoin and this prompted an uncommon drop in its value from $1240 to $576 in only three weeks. Software engineers also decide the usefulness of this worldwide currency and many inquiries the prospect of taking a chance with their funds for some gathering of nerds. This keeps numerous from wandering into the system and expands the danger of the Bitcoin venture profoundly.

What Is Cryptocoin Mining? How Could It Be Useful?

Digital currency is an electronic currency that isn't of a specific country and not created by any administration-controlled bank. These advanced monetary standards are otherwise called Altcoins. They depend on cryptography. This currency is created by a numerical interaction so it won't lose its value because of huge dissemination.

There are various sorts of Crypto Currency like Peercoin, Namecoin, Litecoin, Bitcoin. The exchanges utilizing digital money are done utilizing the system of mining. The people who need to do this cycle, create the money in their PCs with the assistance of the product implied for this reason.

When the currency is made, it is recorded in the company, accordingly reporting its reality. The value of Altcoins went up to astonishing levels during the most recent few years and thus, its mining is currently an exceptionally productive business. Numerous companies began making chips that are solely utilized for running the cryptographic calculations of this interaction. Antminer is a mainstream ASIC equipment utilized for drawing out Bitcoin.

The Bitcoin excavator can procure exchange charges and endowments for the recently made coins. ASIC (Application Specific Integrated Circuit) is a central processor explicitly intended for this interaction. When contrasted with past advancements, they are quicker. The assistance offered by the Bitcoin excavator depends on determined execution. They give a particular degree of creation limit concerning a set cost.

Why You Think Hosting Your Bitcoin Mining Server is Good at Colocation Data Center?

While it is at first savvy to continue to mineworkers in a private or little business setting, the savings immediately decreased as the mining activity increases. Numerous costs are regularly overlooked when a Bitcoin Mining activity fires up. While almost everyone is promptly mindful of the electrical costs associated with the undertaking, covered-up costs rapidly add up. These include:

Cooling Infrastructure Costs: It will take around 40% of the electrical utilization utilized by an excavator to cool the space it is in if mechanical cooling is fundamental. This leaves just 23,040 watts accessible for genuine mining force, and it also adds 40% to the expense of the net power utilized for the activity.

With the public normal of $0.12 per KWh, that carries the complete to $0.16 per Kwh with cooling costs included. Likewise, a net utilization of 23 kW will need about 6.5 extra huge loads of cooling. Most enormous houses have around 6 tons for solace cooling, this will mean an aggregate of 12 tons of cooling important. Introducing this extra forced air system costs currency.

Electrical Infrastructure Costs: Typical new development accommodates a code passable wattage utilization of 38,400 watts. This force figure invalidates the power expected to in reality live or work in the area, and it refutes cooling costs. Introducing around 20 x 20amp power plugs likewise costs currency.

Long Term Opportunity Costs: With the expanding Bitcoin Difficulty, one should consider whether the expenses of introducing 20 x 20amp fittings and 6 extra huge loads of forced air system will make decent long haul speculation. With regards to digital currency and digging for coins, the familiar saying of "time is currency" remains constant like never before. This should be at the bleeding edge of your manner of thinking when choosing how you will approach this interaction. Ensure you pick a server farm that will see how important your uptime is.

Interaction of Mining

Digital currency is cryptographic, which implies that it utilizes extraordinary encryption that permits controlling the age of coins and affirming the exchange. A square is futile in its presently accessible structure. After coordinating, the digger a few bitcoins. For acquiring bitcoin using mining, the digger must be specialized.

Bitcoin digging for benefit is cutthroat. Bitcoin value makes it hard to acknowledge financial additions without also theorizing on the cost. The installment depends on how much their equipment added to settling that puzzle. Diggers check the exchanges, guarantee they aren't bogus, and keep the system murmuring along.

Digital money mining is a computationally serious interaction, which requires a company of a few PCs for confirmation of the exchange record, known as the blockchain. The backhoes are offered a portion of exchange charges and gain a higher likelihood of discovering another square through contributing high computational force. These help exchanges help in giving upgraded security to arrange customers and ensures genuineness, which is dependent upon to be the observable factor influencing the improvement of the worldwide cryptographic money mining market.

Is it possible to mine Bitcoins utilizing Mobile?

Indeed, Bitcoin portable mining is conceivable; yet there are also a few purposes behind not continuing with it. Further, there are not many digital currencies that don't need verification of-work components, which are under the underlying stage can be mined on a cell phone. As we know that the present cell phones are exceptionally amazing and can be utilized for cryptographic money mining.

However, when we analyze the tools that are utilized by the diggers for Bitcoin mining, they are extremely amazing and modern, mining in cell phones implies they have less allure as far as remunerations. The client can mine Bitcoins on the cell phone on a more limited size, or the client can join a versatile mining ranch or mining pool. When the diggers of the company share their prizes, you will get a little rate dependent on your figuring power.

How might you Mine Utilizing Smartphones?

You can utilize your cell phone for Bitcoin versatile mining, by utilizing Android as it is a digging cordial OS for cell phones. As the BTC rate in India is fluctuating, the market is growing more applications for Android, which permits you to simply mine bitcoin from the cell phone. These applications can't be found on the Google play store by and large.

Even though mining through portable doesn't offer more rewards, it's anything but a confounded interaction. The lone prerequisite is, you need a cell phone and download the best mining application. When you are utilizing your cell phone, the application runs behind the scenes; and these applications meddle with your cell phone's exhibition. Compactly, we can say that cell phone mining is one of the simple ways for bringing in some money dislike utilizing specific equipment through PCs.

With no responsibility to anybody, Bitcoins are genuinely interesting. Bitcoins are sovereign with their particular standards and aren't imprinted covertly by any bank yet mined, they're delivered carefully by a decent number of people engaged with a gigantic company or local area. Diggers generally utilize gigantic figuring power, and a lot of rivalries are associated with Bitcoin mining.

The contending diggers also can procure Bitcoins simultaneously, simply by tackling the issue. Although trouble levels of these issues are getting extraordinary step by step. Exchanges at the Bitcoin network are persevering and relentless, and monitoring those exchanges is genuinely orderly.

Bitcoin network keeps it orderly, as, during a given interval of time, all exchanges are gathered in a square. The excavators should approve exchanges, and everything is recorded in an overall record, which is just an assortment of squares, named blockchain. Blockchain holds the way into the subtleties of any exchange made across different Bitcoin addresses.

How to Make Money on Bitcoins?

In case you're as yet doubtful, one Bitcoin is as of now value about $90 (starting at 18 April 2013), with hourly changes that can make an informal investor discombobulated. Unstable, however, an ever-increasing number of people are beginning to drain the wonder for all it is worthwhile it endures. A few different ways: Sell Bitcoin mining PCs, sell your Bitcoins at insane costs on eBay and theorize on Bitcoin markets. You can likewise begin mining.

Any person can mine Bitcoins, yet except if you can bear the cost of a proficient arrangement, it will take a standard PC a year or more to address calculations. A great many people join pools of different excavators who consolidate their registering power for quicker code-breaking.

Conclusion:

Bitcoin advertising is getting fundamental for associations that are conveying administrations to the clients on the loose. Then there are makers of merchandise and things that convey products in return for Bitcoin. They likewise need to have an advertising arrangement at removal as it will balance out the selling cost and thereby making trust society.

A lot of things are occurring in the energizing universe of Bitcoin as many people are bringing in currency trading the digital currency. A few merchants accept that selling Bitcoin online or selling Bitcoin in person is the best thing for any dealer. In any case, every choice enjoys its benefits and drawbacks when figuring out how to exchange Bitcoin.

Purchasing and selling Bitcoin online is by a wide margin the more normal method of trading your Bitcoin. There are presently three ways to selling Bitcoin online. As indicated by certain brokers it should be known at merchants that the costs fall steeply and the dealer may endure enormous misfortunes while selling BTC. This is the straightforward cycle of figuring out how to exchange Bitcoin for benefits.

Pushing products to the individual buyer through the sales rep is a sluggish and costly strategy. Likewise, the quantity of calls is restricted as significant time is taken up in voyaging. In any case, with Bitcoin advertising, it very well may be done successfully as it gives a nearly more affordable strategy.

It should likewise be clarified that in the event of changes in the products, advertising help in giving the essential data rapidly to the clients. Hence, regardless of whether an organization is a maker or an administration supplier, it should utilize Bitcoin advertising for the greatest effect. The effect brings more business and opportunities for the association too.

Bitcoin is making incredible advances into the best trading resources. Reading the live Bitcoin news today you can get thoughts on where the costs are going. Globalization is one of the significant and fragile systems needed for each created agricultural nation as are the idea of Bitcoin and the possibility of the technology.

TRADING

The ultimate guide you need to learn about trading and Becoming a Successful Trader

Introduction

The correct investment strategy can probably be the best pathway to independence from the rat race. Regardless of whether it fills in as an enhancement to your ordinary pay, extra reserve funds for retirement, or an approach to take care of obligation — the best investment procedures can affect your monetary wellbeing to improve things.

That being said, there are countless such sorts of investment systems that can appear to be overpowering from the start. From stocks and bonds to land, there are various alternatives accessible. The accompanying aide will cover a couple of amateur cordial investment procedures and help you track down an ideal choice for your circumstance and objectives. Continue to peruse to find out additional. Start by opening an IRA; at that point, grow your investments utilizing file assets and ETFs, and contribute close to 10% of your portfolio in organization stocks. For some Americans, a business-supported 401(k) is their first investment vehicle, with 65% of U.S. laborers offered one or a similar arrangement. Yet, to fabricate abundance, you additionally may need or have to contribute outside of that arrangement. The best thing about contributing procedures is that they're adaptable. On the off chance that you pick one and it doesn't precisely measure up for your danger resilience or timetable, you can make changes. Be that as it may be cautioned: doing so can be costly. Each buy conveys a charge. All the more critically, selling resources can make an acknowledged capital addition. These increases are available and, in this way, costly.

Here, we take a gander at four regular contributing techniques that suit most financial backers. By setting aside the effort to comprehend the attributes of every, you will be in an ideal situation to pick one that is ideal for you over the long haul without the need to bring about the cost of shifting direction. A typical fantasy about contributing is that multiple ledgers are required to begin. In actuality, the way toward building a solid portfolio can start with a couple thousand—or even two or three hundred—dollars.

This story offers explicit counsel, coordinated by the sum you may have access to start your investments. To begin with, be that as it may, it covers some shrewd moves low-rollers can make to launch a reserve fund and investment program. To start contributing, pick a strategy dependent on the sum you'll contribute, the courses of events for your investment objectives, and the measure of hazard that bodes well for you. Lease, service charges, obligation installments, and staple goods may seem like everything you can bear the cost of when you're simply beginning. Be that as it may, whenever you've dominated planning for those month-to-month costs (and put away, at any rate, a little money in a backup stash), it's an ideal opportunity to begin contributing. The exciting part is sorting out what to put resources into — and how much.

As an amateur to the universe of contributing, you'll have a lot of inquiries, not the least of which is: How would I begin, and what are the best investment techniques for fledgelings? Our guide will respond to those inquiries, and that's just the beginning.

Before you start to explore your investment strategy, it's critical to accumulate some fundamental data about your financial circumstance. Ask yourself these essential inquiries:

- What is your present financial circumstance?

- What is your typical cost for essential items, including month-to-month expenses and obligations?

- What amount would you be able to bear to contribute—both at first and on a continuous premise?

Even though you needn't bother with a great deal of money to begin, you shouldn't start on the off chance that you can't stand to do as such. On the off chance that you have many obligations or different commitments, consider the effect contributing will have on your circumstance before you begin setting money to the side.

Then, put out your objectives. Everybody has various necessities, so you ought to figure out what yours are. Is it true that you are proposing to put something aside for retirement? It is safe to say that you are hoping to make enormous buys like a home or vehicle later on? Or on the other hand, would you say you are putting something aside for your kids' schooling? This will help you restricted down a strategy.

Sort out what your danger resistance is. This is ordinarily controlled by a few key elements, including your age, pay, and how long you have until you resign. The more youthful you are, the more danger you can take on. More danger implies better yields, while lower hazard implies the increases will not be acknowledged as fast. However, remember, high-hazard investments likewise mean there's a more prominent potential for misfortunes also.

At long last, gain proficiency with the fundamentals. It's a smart thought to have a fundamental comprehension of what you're getting into so you're not contributing aimlessly. Pose inquiries. Furthermore, read on to find out about a portion of the vital methodologies out there.

Worth financial backers are deal customers. They look for stocks they accept are underestimated. They search at stocks with costs they accept don't completely mirror the natural worth of the security. Worth contributing is predicated, partially, on the possibility that some level of mindlessness exists on the lookout. This silliness, in principle, presents freedoms to get a stock at a limited cost and bring in money from it.

It's excessive for esteem financial backers to search over volumes of financial information to discover bargains. A large number of significant worth common subsidizes allow financial backers the opportunity to claim a bushel of stocks thought to be underestimated. The Russell 1000 Value Index, for instance, is a famous benchmark for esteem financial backers and a few shared assets impersonate this record.

As examined above, financial backers can change techniques whenever however doing as such—particularly as a worth financial backer—can be expensive. Regardless of this, numerous financial backers abandon the strategy following a couple of poor-performing years. In 2014, Wall Street Journal correspondent Jason Zweig clarified, "Over the course of the decade finished December 31, esteem reserves gaining practical experience in huge stocks returned a normal of 6.7% yearly. However, the average financial backer in those assets acquired simply 5.5% annually."1 Why did this occur? Since such a large number of financial backers chose to haul their money out and run. The exercise here is that to make esteem contributing work, you should play the long game.

You most likely haven't considered purchasing a stock purchasing stock. Most Millennial financial backers don't. Examines have shown that Millennial financial backers are inactive in their investment strategy. You may, in general, support things like your 401(k) or file reserves due to their straightforwardness. However, this isn't generally the most thoughtful approach to contribute.

Worth contributing is clever contributing. I'll utilize the terms conversely in this article. Worth putting centres around putting resources into a quality organization that you believe is underestimated. You settle on this choice dependent on solid essential examination.

It's a purchase and-hold strategy. It focuses on market eruptions to recent developments and to which organizations deliver profits. This leaves a few organizations underestimated, dependent on their drawn-out development potential.

Benjamin Graham is the creator of The Intelligent Investor. In certain circles, he's known as the "Father of Value Investing."

He says that astute financial backers perform total and top to bottom investigations before contributing. Doing this will give them protected and consistent profits from their investments.

They centre around evaluating, as well. Savvy financial backers possibly purchase a stock when its cost is underneath its natural worth.

The characteristic worth is the way you esteem the organization dependent on your major investigation. You do this while disregarding the market. As such, I fail to remember what every other person is saying.

Keen financial backers additionally search for an edge of wellbeing before purchasing a stock. This implies you believe there's a hole between what you'll pay for the supply and what you'll acquire from the store as the organization develops.

To recap, esteem contributing spotlights on:

- Solid central investigation

- Finding and purchasing stocks that are underestimated

- Purchasing with an edge of security

The three principles of value investing

1. Do your exploration

Set aside some effort to dissect and comprehend the organization you are putting resources into before purchasing any stock. You ought to understand the accompanying things about the organization:

- its long-term plans

- it's business principles

- its financial structure

- the group that oversees it (the CEO, CFO, and so forth)

Worth contributing spots attention on organizations that deliver reliable profits. Why? Develop, productive organizations regularly take care of part of their benefits to their financial backers. This piece of the service is known as a profit.

Keen financial backers consistently look past an organization's momentary income also. They don't mind if the organization is well known in the media.

2. Enhance

At any point, hear the expression "don't tie up your resources in one place"? All things considered, it applies to esteem contributing, as well.

Shrewd financial backers have various kinds of investments in their portfolios. This shields them from genuine misfortunes. Even though worth contributing has been demonstrated to bring to the table consistent yearly returns, it's not ensured.

3. Search for protected and consistent (not phenomenal) returns

This one is generally difficult for new financial backers to get a handle on. Everybody needs to bring in money quick. For what reason do you think there are so many "5 Best Stocks for… " articles out there?

In school, I had a class called Advanced Investments. My educator consistently said that assuming you're finding out about a "hot stock," it's now past the point where it is possible to contribute. It bodes well. However, we get tied up with the promotion.

Not many of us need to invest the Momentum and exertion to get protected, consistent returns. We need stocks that will detonate in worth and give remarkable returns. That is not reasonable.

You could discover stocks like that, and it might even keep going for some time. Yet, it will not keep going forever. Sooner or later, that strategy will fizzle.

So as opposed to looking for quick, market-beating returns, clever financial backers need consistency. A canny financial backer will be content with generally safe, predictable profits from their investments after a seemingly endless amount of time after year.

Search for stocks that meet your necessities. Try not to attempt to beat the arrangement of the individuals who do this professionally.

How to get started

Presently it's an ideal opportunity to begin in picking a few stocks. Be that as it may, where would it be a good idea for you to start?

To begin with, you'll need to decide whether you're a cautious financial backer or an ambitious financial backer.

It's typical of a cautious financial backer to:

- hope to diminish hazard as frequently as could be expected

- adopt a more inactive strategy to dealing with their portfolio

- enhance by putting resources into developing blue-chip stocks just as high-grade bonds

Ambitious financial backers are generally:

- more dynamic in dealing with their investments

- willing to face challenges on more current organizations in the desire for a better yield

- expanded, however, place a heavier load on stocks

There's no incorrect method to contribute. Both can be shrewd financial backers on the off chance that they keep the standards of significant worth contributing.

Whenever you've chosen how you need to contribute, it's an ideal opportunity to begin searching for stocks. While I don't propose you go out and purchase a store quickly, I comprehend your time is significant.

I utilize the Classic Benjamin Graham Stock Screener by Serenity Stocks. This is a phenomenal device to get you headed the correct way in searching for underestimated stocks.

When you discover a few stocks you like, start your examination. I was hoping you could make sure to look at the extra connections I've included after each part. This will help you review anything you're new to.

After you've done your exploration, it's an ideal opportunity to contribute. Make a point to contribute what you're open to losing.

Keep in mind and there are no assurances in contributing—even worth contributing.

Youthful grown-ups enjoy a benefit regarding contributing: Longtime skylines mean you can face more challenge than more seasoned individuals. On the off chance that you are alright with more severe dangers, unfamiliar business sectors are an extraordinary chance to get better yields.

Putting resources into unfamiliar business sectors can be somewhat confounding. They appear to be going here and there constantly, and large crashes worldwide continue to make the news. So for what reason would it be advisable for you to get included?

There are two primary reasons foreign assets will profit both your funds and your mental soundness. They can:

- Expand your investment portfolio

- Permit you to exploit the long haul development potential

Regardless of how developed, each market will go through a progression of ups, downs, and adjustments on a semi-standard premise. Purchasing stocks in unfamiliar business sectors that follow an alternate design than the US adds a layer of safety to your investment. It's simply savvy not to keep all your assets tied up in one place. The US has a developed routinely exchanged investment market. It pushes ahead at a moderately sluggish, consistent speed, which makes it harder to acknowledge enormous additions to your investments. Then again, unfamiliar business sectors, similar to the more youthful economies of Eastern Europe, South America, Africa, Asia, and the Middle East, have tremendous long haul development potential.

Stock costs go here and there—it's precisely what they do. Markets will take short plunges, and economies will stumble into difficulty. This choppiness is imperative to follow on the off chance that you are a stock representative, and your responsibility is to make the present moment risky investments. In any case, when you are working for the future, it doesn't bode well to watch these everyday vacillations.

What are significant are the drawn-out patterns that are not influenced by transient market unpredictability. You care about your future—a stock going here and two or three pennies short-term shouldn't mean a lot to you contrasted with its pattern over numerous years.

ETFs and ease common assets are an excellent method to get the drawn-out advantages of foreign market investment while limiting the transient dangers.

Both work by gathering stocks and markets together. Rather than becoming tied up with a solitary organization that may fail spectacularly, you become tied up with a gathering of organizations that sell an assortment of items and administrations; the variety shields you from momentary misfortunes by engrossing any stun waves.

Most importantly, it's brilliant to get into ETFs or shared assets with low-cost proportions that are adequately different to cover a decent cross-part of the market. There a lot of alternatives to browse, including:

Vanguard Total International Stock ETF (VXUS)

This ETF covers the whole global market outside the US. That is comparably different (and protected) as you can get when contributing universally.

iShares MSCI Pacific ex-Japan (EPP)

This asset is more explicit, covering stocks just in Asia, however barring Japan. The developing business sectors of China and India could give critical development throughout the next few decades.

Vanguard European Stock Index Fund (VEURX)

Morningstar calls this asset "perhaps the most ideal choice for uninvolved openness to European stocks," a financial backer can discover. Even though Europe has encountered unpredictability this decade, that could mean you get the opportunity to purchase low and watch the business sectors settle and fill later on.

Any investment is at any rate somewhat dangerous. Yet, hazard is important to get any opportunity of gains. Unfamiliar business sectors are less secure than US markets, yet they additionally have a higher possibility of developing over the long haul.

Try not to get tricked by the news reports—market variances are characteristic, and make little difference to genuine development throughout extensive stretches of time. Placing the part of your investments in unfamiliar business sectors either through ETFs or ease common assets and playing the long game will augment your opportunity of genuine increases over your lifetime.

Understanding Your Mind Will Make You a Better Investor

You see how your psyche functions will help you improve investments. Find three ideas that clarify how you think — and how that can make you a superior financial backer.

Contributing without seeing how your mind is settling on choices is an exercise in futility. It's likewise a misuse of money.

This post will uncover a couple of influential ideas that will change how you consider contributing. Applying these ideas will make you a superior financial backer over the long haul.

My failed investment

At the point when I was more youthful, I settled on vast loads of incautious investment choices. Not simply with stocks. I thought it'd be an excellent investment to purchase Teenage Mutant Ninja Turtle activity figures in school. The statistics were as yet in their unique bundling. I figured I'd get them in mass, at that point, auction them individually for tremendous benefits. Good thought, isn't that so?

For reasons unknown, the market for purchasing toys wasn't as I'd anticipated. The more significant part of individuals purchasing figures on eBay were re-merchants like me, wanting to make a speedy buck. So no one was buying. I wound up losing money on the investment, having to exchange the vast majority of the figures in mass for a misfortune.

Thinking back on the investment, I realize it was dumb. It was rash. I didn't do any examination. It didn't bode well. So for what reason did I do it?

You've doubtlessly been in the present circumstance previously. You purchase a stock (or some other kind of investment), and it loses esteem. After you've assumed your misfortune and proceeded onward, you can't help thinking about why you made that investment in any case. Was it somebody's recommendation? Is it true that you were attracted to the organization's items? Did you think you were beating the market?

Nobel Prize champ Daniel Kahneman composed an incredible book called Thinking, Fast and Slow. The book examines the brain science behind how our psyche functions. The exploration in the book applies to contributing, also. We should investigate a portion of the ideas and understand they can make you a superior financial backer.

Concept one: Your two minds

Our brain has two frameworks that interact with data. It influences how we think, concoct choices, act, and judge circumstances. This is urgent when you're contributing. The first is framework one. I like to consider it our "sluggish mind." System 1 is the piece of the cerebrum that responds on instinct. It's hasty and programmed. It's non-cognizant.

For instance, you may purchase stock in an organization since they have a hot new item out. You think it'll change how purchasers carry on. You don't want to delve into the organization's financials or history immediately. Your framework one brain is attracted to the story and leads you to make an indiscreet, apathetic choice.

To clarify this somewhat further, I'll utilize the model from the book:

A bat and a ball cost $1.10. The bat costs a dollar more than the ball. What amount does the ball cost?

Without a doubt, you said a dime. This is your framework one working; however, it's mistaken. On the off chance that you pause for a minute to figure it out, you'll see that the appropriate response is five pennies. So what was the deal? Your framework one depended without really thinking to respond to the inquiry you thought was basic.

How should this influence your investment choices?

The following kind is framework two, and it's more cognizant. It requires exertion. It's the piece of our mind that will permit us to concentrate. We would then be able to make intentional, thought-out choices. Yet, it additionally necessitates that you put your motivations away and focus.

We should look again at the model above. If you're utilizing your framework two, you may settle on an alternate choice on the stock. You may prevent yourself from purchasing the store in the wake of dissecting the organization's financials. Or on the other hand, you may see they have numerous contenders and a little unreasonable net revenue.

My framework one was the essential driver of my investment in Ninja Turtles activity figures. I purchased the figures without much forethought. I disregarded the expenses. I missed the likely absence of benefit. This was supportive of the appeal of buying and selling toys from my youth.

Train your mind to be less passive and utilize your System two all the more frequently. By doing this, you'll increment the strength of your insight. You'll likewise turn out to be more engaged when you settle on investment choices.

Here are five phenomenal mind preparing applications for you to attempt at this moment:

- Elevate

- Lumosity

- CogniFit

- Peak

- Fit Brains

Concept two: Priming

Preparing is an idea where certain words, pictures, or articles can influence our cerebrum. This affects how you decide.

For instance, when you consider espresso, the top brand or organization, most of us think it is Starbucks. That is because our way of life and society has "prepared us" to do as such. Wherever we look, we see logos and advertisements for Starbucks. We see individuals on TV drinking Starbucks while strolling through New York City. This is preparing us to make a relationship to espresso when we see or hear certain words.

Suppose you need to put resources into an espresso organization. Utilizing the model above, you may consider Starbucks the best investment. Yet, this could be because of the preparation you've encountered. You may think Starbucks is the best investment since everybody drinks it. You may likewise connect Starbucks with New

York and New York with abundance. This may make you look past a more modest espresso organization that is a superior investment.

Preparing is a typical result of the way of life we live in. It pushes us to settle on investment decisions we may think nothing about. It happens constantly, yet we do it without knowing.

Examination of the organization and its industry top to bottom before contributing. Moderate down and think (utilize your framework two) preceding heading out to get one of the "10 Hottest Stocks for Christmas." You may be getting prepared.

Here are two of the best assets for finding out about an organization:

- EDGAR Database: the financial information for any traded on an open market organization

- Yahoo! Finance and Yahoo! Account Markets: both incredible assets for getting familiar with your organization, its rivals, and the market it is in

Concept three: Snap decisions and misrepresentation

Two fundamental ideas can influence how you pick investments. The first is the corona impact. This is your brain's languid propensity to relate two irrelevant things. It tends to be an individual, item, or circumstance and is generally a consequence of a past idea or information point you have.

For instance: You own an iPhone, MacBook, and iPad. You're an Apple enthusiast, and you love their items. Along these lines (and this lone), you believe that Apple would make the best vehicles. However, because they make fantastic hardware doesn't mean they would make superb vehicles.

The subsequent idea is the affirmation inclination. This one is difficult and happens regularly. It's the propensity for us to concur with opinions and conclusions that are following our convictions.

For example, suppose that you feel that Miller Lite is a decent brew. Suppose I am a renowned brewmaster. If I revealed to you that Miller Lite was the best brew, however, it was likewise helpful for you, you would concur with me. Without a doubt, you'd currently feel that Miller Lite was the best lager, not simply a decent brew. I, the master, presently affirmed your assessment.

Kow your organization all around; at that point, structure your assessment. Utilize the assets from idea two as a benchmark. At that point, make it a stride further by taking a gander at the other top to bottom examination. See things like a stock's danger rating, verifiable information and patterns, and investigator's examination reports.

Here are three all-around regarded premium stock exploration locales for you to investigate:

- Morningstar

- Zacks Premium

- S&P Capital IQ

Toward the day's end, you need to choose how significant contributions is to you. It is safe to say that you are OK with making sluggish, imprudent choices? Or on the other hand, would you rather invest a little Momentum and exertion to settle on a more good choice?

Regardless of whether you're putting resources into Zhu Pets or stocks and bonds, understanding these ideas (and applying methods to make your cerebrum work for you) will make you a superior financial backer over the long haul.

Warren Buffet: The Ultimate Value Investor

In any case, in the event that you are a genuine worth financial backer, you needn't bother with anybody to persuade you to have to remain in it for the since quite a while ago run since this strategy is planned around the possibility that one should purchase organizations—not stocks. That implies the financial backer should think about the 10,000 foot view, not an impermanent knockout execution. Individuals regularly refer to unbelievable financial backer Warren Buffet as the encapsulation of a worth financial backer. He gets his work done— some of the time for quite a long time. Yet, when he's prepared, he bets everything and is submitted as long as possible.

Consider Buffett's words when he made a significant investment in the carrier business. He clarified that aircrafts "had an awful first century." Then he said, "And they moved a terrible century, I hope."2 This reasoning embodies a significant part of the worth contributing methodology. Decisions depend on many years of patterns and in light of many years of future execution.

Worth Investing Tools

For the individuals who don't have the opportunity to perform comprehensive examination, the value income proportion (P/E) has become the essential instrument for rapidly recognizing underestimated or modest stocks. This is a solitary number that comes from isolating a stock's offer cost by its profit per share (EPS). A lower P/E proportion implies you're paying less per $1 of current profit. Worth financial backers look for organizations with a low P/E proportion.

While utilizing the P/E proportion is a decent beginning, a few specialists caution this estimation alone isn't sufficient to make the strategy work. Exploration distributed in the Financial Analysts Journal confirmed that "Quantitative investment procedures dependent on such proportions are bad substitutes for esteem contributing methodologies that utilization an exhaustive methodology in recognizing undervalued protections." The explanation, as per their work, is that financial backers are frequently tricked by low P/E proportion stocks dependent on incidentally expanded bookkeeping numbers. These low figures are, in numerous occasions, the aftereffect of a dishonestly high income figure (the denominator). At the point when genuine income are accounted for (not simply guage) they're frequently lower. This outcomes in a "inversion to the mean." The P/E proportion goes up and the worth the financial backer sought after is gone.

On the off chance that utilizing the P/E proportion alone is defective, how should a financial backer deal with discover genuine worth stocks? The analysts recommend, "Quantitative ways to deal with distinguishing these twists—like joining predictable worth with Momentum, quality and productivity measures—can help in keeping away from these 'esteem traps.'"

In this day and age, we need everything improved.

The PC age has made us so subject to innovation. In a manner, it's acceptable because we would now be able to zero in on our work and let our devices do the challenging work. The accompanying rundown is sites to help you research quicker and deal with your money better.

That way, you can put your consideration on the principal thing;

- time
- loved ones
- building riches

Alert: don't burn through a lot of time going through each site. It's ideal to utilize the locales that will profit your style of exploration. NOT to sit around messing with everything. It's so natural to turn upward and understand an hour has passed and everything you've done is surf the web.

So right away, here are the best contributing and money instruments to assist you with completing things quicker.

Earnings Cast

Veteran financial backers realize that tuning in to income call can give critical contributing understanding. You can distinguish whether the supervisory group is over hopeful, regardless of whether they are straight talkers or more like sales reps.

Trefis

This site fundamentally assists clients with dissecting the income streams for the organizations that are covered. Rather than simply seeing a solitary number that addresses income, you can perceive how it is separated.

Likewise, you can change the development of income sections to think of new valuations for what the stock would be worth.

Estimize

Estimize is the place where you can look at what individuals are expecting the EPS gauge to be. It's generally for subsequent quarter profit; however, the area of the site is to show how better standard people can assess EPS over investigators.

Street of Walls

This site is for individuals searching for work in Wallstreet. However, their preparation area is magnificent for instruction.

The site gives preparing to help you become top ability paying little heed to your experience.

Before you plunge into the meat of the substance, if you haven't joined with your email for our free investment assets, do as such.

I'll quickly send you additional stock proportions notes, agendas, accounting pages and other downloads you can prevail with.

Mint

Mint is extraordinary to keep an idea about your accounting records. Contributing is magnificent, and yet, it's likewise essential to hold your budgets within proper limits.

With XBRL, numerous organizations are coming out with approaches to make SEC filings and search simpler and better.

The solitary blow is that the US House of Representatives has passed a bill where organizations making under $250m in income are not needed to record utilizing XBRL.

Rank and Filed

It very well may be exceptionally overwhelming and tedious with regards to perusing the SEC records. Rank and Filed is a great site to make perusing Sec filings simpler.

This is what Rank and Filed are in their own words:

It resembles the SEC's EDGAR data set, yet for people.

BamSEC

This is a charge based assistance yet must be incorporated because it's clean thus simple to utilize. Enter a ticker into their pursuit bar, and you'll get a rundown of the relative multitude of filings in a simple to peruse and look through design.

Finviz

Heaps of market information and perceptions. Far superior to the more significant part of the other more excellent account destinations.

You can peruse all accessible stock information. There are channels, signals and stock screens you can use to filter through all the data.

Morningstar

Excellent site for stock examination, five years of free financial information and basics.

The articles are superior to most locales, yet they centre around generally huge covers.

gurufocus

GuruFocus.com is a quality worth contributing site offering heaps of information and investigation and spot an extraordinary accentuation on what the "master" financial backers are doing and holding.

Top Asset Management Tools

The pattern in money these days is mechanized portfolio the executives. For individuals who need an uninvolved technique for contributing, this is presumably the ideal approach to minor expenses.

SigFig

They rebranded their site. It used to be a pink pig all over the place; however, they've exchanged their plan of action to be more centred around auto portfolio the executives.

Money never dozes, and neither do we. Our unprejudiced calculations are continually observing your investments, giving a fair portfolio customized only for you.

You can likewise connect up your money market funds to follow execution and other details.

Personal Capital

One of the new and hot resources the board devices available. You don't need to pursue any paid administrations, yet you'll get calls once in a while to join their portfolio of the executive's administration.

Yet, if you contribute all alone, utilizing their portfolio apparatus isn't so awful.

At the point when you become an investment customer, we'll match you with a group of guides who will become acquainted with you, your novel financial circumstance, and your objectives.

Advancement

Same as the other two; however, I trust Betterment has been around longer.

Another decision to handily deal with your portfolio and put it on autopilot.

Put resources into a broadened arrangement of stock and bond ETFs intended for ideal anticipated returns.

You will set aside time and cash since everything is robotized with a low administration charge.

Bloomberg Visual Data

From MLB groups esteem, the 2014 World Cup, and tycoons record, Bloomberg visual information gives you a graphic portrayal of data making it drawing in and more apparent.

It's as yet youthful, yet the substance is vibrant, and you can undoubtedly comprehend the information, which would be inconceivable if it was recorded on a table.

XBRL

A representation apparatus from the XBRL consortium to show which organizations and enterprises have recorded with the SEC.

XBRL has been moving for quite a while and is developing; in any case, it endured a new shot when the House of Representatives declared that organizations with under $250m in income don't need to record utilizing XBRL.

That is 60% of all open organizations. We'll perceive how XBRL defeats this. Up to that point, it is anything but innovation to depend 100% on.

TradingView

This simple to-utilize diagramming site will give you continuous data and necessary market experiences—incredible programming for diagrams.

The best on the web stock graphs and a local area of financial backers who are energetic about sharing exchanging thoughts.

With only a single tick, you can see live graphs and explained articles put together by local area individuals.

StockCharts

It still has a burdensome mid-2000 UI, yet it works and is quite possibly the most famous destination for outlines if you're into the specialized examination.

Who figured making top-notch financial outlines could be so natural? We have the apparatuses, instructive data, well-qualified suppositions, and backing you need to comprehend the business sectors. Recall that while anybody can utilize our free instruments, just endorsers approach our most impressive highlights.

What's the Message?

The message here is that worth contributing can work insofar as the financial backer is in it as long as possible and is set up to apply some genuine exertion and examination to their stock determination. Those willing to place the work in and stay remain to acquire. One investigation from Dodge and Cox discovered that esteem procedures almost consistently beat development methodologies "over skylines of 10 years or more." The examination proceeds to clarify that esteem systems have failed to meet expectations development techniques for a 10-year time span in only three periods in the course of the most recent 90 years. Those periods were the Great Depression (1929-

1939/40), the Technology Stock Bubble (1989-1999), and the period 2004-2014/15.

Strategy 2: Growth Investing

Maybe then search for ease bargains; financial development backers need investments that offer solid potential gain potential regarding the future income of stocks. It very well may be said that a development financial backer is regularly searching for the "following huge thing." Growth contributing, nonetheless, is anything but a foolish hug of theoretical contributing. Maybe, it includes assessing a stock's present wellbeing just as its capability to develop.

A development financial backer considers the possibilities of the business wherein the stock flourishes. You may ask, for instance, if there's a future for electric vehicles before putting resources into Tesla. Or then again, you may contemplate whether A.I. will turn into an installation of ordinary living before putting resources into an innovation organization. There should be proof of an endless and hearty hunger for the organization's administrations or items if it will develop. Financial backers can address this inquiry by taking a gander at an organization's new history. Basically: A development stock ought to be growing. The organization ought to have a reliable pattern of solid profit and income, meaning an ability to follow through on development assumptions.

A downside to development contributing is an absence of profits. On the off chance that an organization is in development mode, it frequently needs funding to support its extension. This doesn't leave a lot (or any) cash left for profit installments. In addition, with quicker profit development comes higher valuations which are, for most financial backers, a higher danger recommendation.

93

As the examination above demonstrates, esteem contributing will, in general, beat development contributing over the long haul. These discoveries don't mean a development financial backer can't benefit from the strategy; it simply implies a development strategy doesn't usually create the degree of profits seen with esteem contributing. However, as per an investigation from New York University's Stern School of Business, "While development contributing fails to meet expectations esteem contributing, particularly throughout long time-frames, it is additionally evident that there are sub-periods, where development contributing dominates." The test is deciding when these "sub-periods" will happen.

Strangely, deciding the periods when a development strategy is ready to perform may mean taking a gander at the total national output (GDP). Take the time somewhere in the range of 2000 and 2015, when a development strategy beat a worth plan in seven years. During five of these years, the GDP development rate was underneath 2%. Then, a worth approach won in nine years, and in seven of those years, the GDP was above 2%. Consequently, it makes sense that a development strategy might be more effective during times of diminishing GDP.

Some development contributing style doubters caution that "development at any cost" is a risky methodology. Such a drive brought about the tech bubble, which disintegrated a large number of portfolios. "Absurd decade, the normal development stock has returned 159% versus only 89% for esteem," as indicated by Money magazine's Investor's Guide 2018.

Stock market contributing isn't close to as messy as many Wall Street experts would have you accept. Actually, by applying a reliable methodology that praises a couple of key financial standards - like broadening, judiciousness, and long haul thinking - anybody can assemble a portfolio custom-made to their specific retirement objectives.

Development contributing is perhaps the most mainstream styles out there, and here we'll investigate the means associated with exploiting this strategy.

What is growth investing?

To start with, it's useful to comprehend what development contributing is - and what it isn't. The methodology alludes to purchasing stocks connected to organizations that have alluring qualities their opponents need. These can incorporate effectively quantifiable things, for example, market-beating development rates in deals or potentially profit. Likewise, they can contain more subjective factors like solid client unwavering ness, a significant brand, or many deep canals.

Development stocks will, in general, stand firm on good footings in arising industry specialities that component long runways for extension in front of them. Because of this alluring potential and the strangely solid achievement, the business has had. Lately, a development stock is evaluated at a top-notch that mirrors the idealism financial backers have in the organization. Thus, the least difficult approach to realize whether you're taking a gander at a development stock is if its valuation, generally its cost to-profit numerous, is high compared with the more extensive market and its industry peers.

This methodology appears differently about esteem contributing, which centres around stocks that have become undesirable on Wall Street. These are stocks with lower valuations that reflect more unassuming deals and benefit possibilities. Both investment procedures can work whenever applied reliably. However, financial backers, for the most part, incline toward one side of the range or the other.

So since you realize development contributing is for you, we should investigate the means engaged with completely benefiting from the strategy.

Step 1: Prepare your finances.

A decent dependable guideline is that you shouldn't accept stocks with the cash you get you'll require in the following five years at any rate. That is because while the market, for the most part, ascends over the long haul, it as often as possible posts sharp drops of 10%, 20%, or more that happen abruptly. Probably the greatest mix-up you can make as a financial backer is setting yourself in a place to be compelled to sell stocks during one of these down periods. In a perfect world, you'll rather be prepared to purchase supplies when most others are selling.

Step 2: Get comfortable with growth approaches.

Presently that you're on the way toward more grounded funds, it's an ideal opportunity to arm yourself with another useful asset: information. There are a couple of kinds of development contributing techniques you can decide to follow.

For instance, you can zero in just on huge, grounded organizations that, as of now, have a background marked by producing positive income. Your methodology could be moored in quantitative measurements that fit in stock screeners, like working edge, return on contributed capital and yearly compound development. Then again, numerous development financial backers mean to buy the best-performing organizations around, as proven by their steady market share gains, with to lesser degree attention on share costs.

It regularly bodes well to centre your buys in enterprises and organizations you know especially well. Regardless of whether that is because you have insight in, say, the eatery business or in working for a cloud programming administrations business, that information will assist you with assessing investments as potential purchase up-and-comers. It's generally desirable to know a ton about a little fragment of organizations than to see slightly about a wide scope of organizations.

However, what is basic to your profits is that you reliably apply the strategy you pick and stay away from the compulsion to hop, starting with one methodology then onto the next, basically because all accounts work better right now. That technique is classified as "pursuing returns," and it's a certain method to fail to meet expectations of the market over the long haul.

Keep away from that destiny by getting comfortable with the fundamentals of this stock market contributing strategy. Perusing a couple of moral development donating books is an incredible spot to begin, and afterwards, familiarize yourself with the bosses in the field.

For instance, T. Rowe Price is credited similar to the dad of development contributing, and, even though he resigned from the field in 1971, his impact is as yet being felt today. Cost advocated the possibility that an organization's profit development could be projected out over numerous years, which moved financial backers' intuition when stocks were viewed as repeating, momentary investments.

Warren Buffett is typically portrayed as a worth financial backer, yet components of his methodology are of the development assortment. This statement from Buffett is an exemplary enunciation of the strategy: "It's far superior to purchase an awesome organization at a reasonable cost than a reasonable organization at a brilliant cost." all in all, the cost is a significant piece of any investment; however the strength of the business ostensibly matters similarly to such an extent, if not more.

Step 3: Stock selection

Presently it's an ideal opportunity to plan to start making investments. This piece of the interaction begins with choosing exactly how much money you need to designate toward your development investment strategy. If you're shiny new to the methodology, it may bode well to begin a little with, say, 10% of your portfolio reserves. As you get more familiar with the instability and develop experience contributing through various sorts of markets (rallies, droops, and everything in the middle), this proportion can rise.

Hazard assumes a major part in this decision, as well, since development stocks are viewed as more Momentumful, and subsequently, more unstable than guarded stocks. That is why a more extended time skyline by and large permits greater adaptability to lean your portfolio toward this contributing style.

A decent method to check whether you have excessively high distribution toward development stocks is if your portfolio makes you restless. On the off chance that you wind up stressed over likely misfortunes or worrying over past market drops, you should lessen your openness to singular development stocks for more various choices.

Buying growth funds

The simplest method to acquire openness to a different scope of development stocks is through an asset. Numerous retirement plans highlight development centred choices, and these could shape the premise of your contributing strategy.

Venturing farther into self-coordinated decisions, consider buying a development based list store. File reserves are ideal investment vehicles since they convey broadening at lower costs than with shared assets. In contrast to common assets controlled by investment administrators who attempt to beat the market, file finances use PC calculations to match the arrival of the business benchmark. Since most investment chiefs miss the mark concerning that benchmark, you'll typically wind up on top of things with a file store.

Index Fund	Annual Expense	Turnover
Vanguard Growth Index Fund	0.17%	6%
SPDR S&P 500 Growth ETF	0.04%	20%

iShares Russell 1000 Growth ETF	0.2%	13%

If you'd prefer to move into the DIY domain, you can purchase singular development stocks. This methodology has the highest potential for market-beating returns, yet it likewise conveys considerably more danger than putting resources into a differentiated asset.

To discover development stocks, screen for elements, for example, these:

- Better than expected development in income per share or the benefits the organization produces every year.

- Better than expected benefit (working edge or gross edge), or the level of deals an organization transforms into services.

- High authentic development in income or deals.

- The exceptional yield on contributed capital is a proportion of how effectively an organization goes through its money.

Simultaneously, you'll need to keep an eye out for warnings that raise the hazard of a business. A couple of models:

- The organization booked a yearly total deficit in the previous three years. This isn't a major issue for most development financial backers, yet it recommends an organization presently can't seem to fabricate a manageable plan of action.

- The organization conveys a low market capitalization (of, for instance, underneath $500 million). Small stocks are powerless against greater contenders and numerous different interruptions that could undermine their whole organizations.

Thus, countless financial backers feel good starting their inquiry in the "mid-cap" scope of stocks.

- There was a new administration purge, especially in the CEO position.

- Deals or potentially productivity is falling. It will not qualify as a development stock if its centre working measurements are going lower.

Step 4: Maximize returns.

Development stocks will, in general, be unpredictable, and keeping in mind that your point ought to be to hold every investment for at least quite a while, you'll, in any case, need to watch out for critical estimating changes for a couple of key reasons.

On the off chance that a segment of your property has acquired such an excess of significant worth that it overwhelms your portfolio, it may bode well to diminish your openness by rebalancing your portfolio.

On the off chance that a stock transcends your gauge of its worth, you can think about selling it, particularly if you've recognized other, all the more sensibly valued investments to coordinate the assets toward.

If the organization has hit a tough situation that has broken your unique investment theory or explained you purchased the stock in any case, you should sell. A wrecked postulation may incorporate significant stumbles by the supervisory crew, a drawn-out decrease in estimating Momentum, or disturbance by a lower-evaluated contender.

These are only a portion of the numerous reasons a financial backer should make changes by their portfolio by choosing to sell a stock.

Accepting you got your work done when you at first bought your stocks, as a rule, your work will add up to standing by, being patient, and permitting the Momentum of intensifying re-visitations of development to its full effect on your portfolio throughout the following 10, 20, or 30 years and that's just the beginning.

Investing in Hot Sectors

One methodology development financial backers can take is to put resources into stocks, common assets, and ETFs dependent on explicit areas and businesses. The achievement of organizations in different regions changes over the long haul. Notwithstanding, it's typically genuinely simple to recognize areas that are "hot" in the feeling of creating better than expected returns for traded on an open market organization.

For instance, two areas that have been especially hot for years and years are medical services and innovation. Organizations that manage innovation, mechanical advances, or are continually putting out new equipment, programming, and gadgets are good picks for financial development backers. The equivalent is valid for organizations in the medical care area. Consider it consistently: Everyone, sooner or later, necessities to focus on their wellbeing, and some organizations are continually growing new prescriptions, treatments, medicines, and places to go to get to this consideration. The medical care area will probably keep getting a charge out of fast development as it serves a maturing child of post-war America age. Indeed, these two areas are connected, as numerous new mechanical improvements have been propelling in medical services innovation.

Development financial backers can work on area contributing by exploiting investment vehicles, such as common assets and ETFs containing a bin of stocks connected to explicit regions. ETFs are an inexorably mainstream investment alternative because of their overall liquidity and lower exchange costs compared to shared assets.

Understanding Earnings

For financial development backers in stocks, understanding an organization's net income is fundamental. This doesn't mean knowing their present income, yet considering their verifiable profit also since this empowers a financial backer to assess current yield comparative with an organization's previous exhibition. Additionally, investigating an organization's income history gives a clearer sign of the organization's likelihood of producing higher future profit.

A high-profit execution in a given quarter or year may address a one-time oddity in an organization's presentation, a proceeding with the pattern, or a specific point in an income cycle that the organization keeps rehashing after some time.

It's additionally imperative to comprehend that even organizations with moderately low, or in some cases even worse, income may, in any case, be a decent pick for a development financial backer. Recollect that profit are what's leftover in the wake of taking away all creation, marketing, working, work, and expense costs from an organization's gross income. On numerous occasions, more modest organizations endeavour to make a forward leap by piping more capital toward developing their business, which may contrarily affect their income in the short run, however over the long haul, creating more significant yields more important benefits for financial backers. In such a circumstance, shrewd financial backers think about different variables, like the nature of an organization's administration, to discover hints concerning the organization's actual development potential.

Growth Investing Through Value Investing

Development financial backers are adequately esteemed financial backers once in a while, in that they search out organizations whose stock might be presently underestimated because of reasons that might be pretty much as straightforward as the way that the organization is moderately new and has not yet grabbed the eye of numerous investment experts or asset directors.

The objective is to get up shares at a low cost of an organization that is very much situated to appreciate a sizeable and proceeded with the flood in development. There are various potential approaches to distinguishing such organizations, one of which we've effectively addressed – taking a gander at organizations in hot areas. Financial backers who can determine another very much oversaw and all around supported organization essential for a desirable location can frequently receive significant benefits. Another conceivable methodology is to inspect organizations on the downslope; for example, those who have gone through insolvency or redesign will probably endure and recuperate.

Using the Price-to-Earnings Ratio

The value/profit (P/E) proportion is an apparatus that financial development backers regularly use to help them pick stocks to put resources into. As the proportion's name makes apparent, you need to comprehend an organization's profit before you can adequately utilize the instrument.

As a rule, the higher the P/E proportion, the more prominent the danger financial backers will take on an organization due to its projected income and development rate.

The P/E proportion is especially valuable for financial development backers attempting to look at organizations that work in a similar industry. In set up businesses and areas, there will, in general, be normal P/E proportions for that specific industry or size. Knowing such industry or area midpoints makes an organization's P/E balance a considerably more helpful number than essentially viewing it in contrast with the market in general.

Taking a gander at an organization's P/E proportion stays a valuable logical device for financial development backers; however, adding thought of another key economic measurement can assist with fining tune your investment picks.

Using the Price-to-Book Ratio

The cost to-book proportion – or P/B proportion – is frequently viewed as more the essential scientific measurement of significant worth financial backers than financial development backers. Nonetheless, the truth of the matter is that the P/B proportion can likewise be used as a powerful apparatus in recognizing stocks with high development potential.

The P/B proportion is determined by separating a stock's for every offer cost by the book esteem per share. To decide the book worth of stock, the favoured stock that has been given should be deducted from the all-out stockholder value. All introductory offers should then partition the figure determined from this takeaway as yet exceptional. The last number is the organization's book esteem per portion of the stock. It is frequently useful for financial backers, particularly development financial backers, to contrast an organization's book esteem with its market esteem. This examination can give a decent sign of whether a stock is underestimated or exaggerated. Organizations with high development potential are habitually underestimated because of heftier obligation burdens and capital consumptions.

How about we put this proportion to utilize. For this model, we will use the S&P 500 Index. A development financial backer would, in principle, investigate the entirety of the stocks, computing or looking into the P/B proportion for each. Notwithstanding how the stores are recorded, the development financial backer could improve them as indicated by their P/B ratio, beginning with the most important numbers and finishing with the least. The organizations that fall inside the top third of the rundown would be viewed as possibly great development stock picks. Remember that this is certainly not an exact science yet, to a greater extent, an accommodating model that financial development backers can utilize to distinguish and add stocks with the best potential for development to their portfolios.

High-Risk Growth Investments

Development putting may likewise reach out into investments past customary stock market contributing.

Putting resources into high-hazard development investments – likewise alluded to as speculative investments – is a methodology that isn't appropriate for financial backers with a low edge for hazard. This strategy is most suitable for economic development backers searching for the greatest benefits inside a generally brief timeframe casing and who have adequate investment money to support them during potential times of misfortunes.

High-hazard investments incorporate such things as fates, alternatives contracts, foreign cash trade (forex), penny stocks, and theoretical land, for example, land that hasn't been created. These investments imply more danger in that they offer no ensured return. Their worth will, in general, change rapidly (at the end of the day, they're dependent upon more noteworthy unpredictability). In any case, the draw for some financial backers is that when such investments pay off, they frequently pay off huge.

In case you're thinking about any of these investments, recollect that exploration is critical to progress. More so than the normal stock or bond financial backer, you need to realize the market you're putting resources into well indeed. Since progress depends greatly on theory, we unequivocally suggest that lone experienced financial backers roll the dice on investment resources, for example, these.

A couple of fundamental classifications of resources have verifiably shown the best development potential. Every one of them includes the value in some structure, and they generally accompany a more significant level of hazard. Individuals have a wide range of styles and tastes regarding money, yet bringing in your money development is normally viewed as the most basic investment objective. The ideal approach to achieve this objective will differ as per factors like the financial backer's danger resilience and time skyline. In any case, there are some key standards and procedures that are material to a wide range of kinds of financial backers and development systems.

Kinds of development investments incorporate the accompanying:

Small-Cap Stocks

The size of an organization depends on its market capitalization or total assets. There is no careful, widespread meaning of what is viewed as a "little cap" contrasted with miniature, mid or huge cap. Yet, most examiners characterize any organization with a capitalization of between $300 million and $2 billion as a little cap firm.

Organizations in this classification are generally still in their underlying period of development, and their stocks have the potential for generous appreciation in cost. Little cap stocks usually have posted more significant yields than their blue-chip cousins, yet they are likewise impressively more unstable and convey a more serious level of hazard. Little cap stocks have additionally frequently beaten enormous cap stocks during times of recovery from downturns.

Technology and Healthcare Stocks

Organizations that grow new advances or offer developments in medical services can be magnificent decisions for financial backers searching for a grand slam play in their portfolios. The stocks of organizations that create famous or progressive items can rise dramatically in cost in a generally brief timeframe.

For instance, the cost of Pfizer (PFE) was just shy of $5 an offer in 1994 preceding Viagra was delivered. This blockbuster drug took the organization's stock cost to above $30 a bid over the following five years on the FDA endorsement of the medication in 1998. Now and again, a development stock can go on a wild ride. Streaming media organization (ROKU) flooded in the months after its first sale of stock (IPO) in the fall of 2017 to withdraw towards the end cost from its first day of exchanging only a couple of short months after the fact.

Speculative Investments

Daredevils and theorists look to high-chance development instruments, for example, penny stocks, fates and alternatives contracts, unfamiliar cash and theoretical land like lacking area. There are additionally oil and gas boring organizations and private value for Momentumful financial backers in big league salary sections. The individuals who pick the correct decisions in this field can see a profit from the capital of commonly their underlying investment; however, they can likewise frequently lose each penny of their head.

Researching Growth Stocks

There are a few key factors that should be viewed while assessing investment development. The pace of development, the sum and kind of hazard and different components of putting assume a great part in the measure of money that financial backers leave with.

With regards to stocks, a portion of the information that financial development backers and experts analyze incorporate the accompanying:

Return on Equity (ROE)

ROE is a numerical articulation of how productively a partnership can make a benefit. It is measured as a rate that addresses the organization's overall gain (which implies the pay staying after the favoured stockholders have been paid, however, before the regular stock profits are paid) separated by the absolute value of the investors.

For instance, if one organization has all out investor value of $100 million while another organization has an investment value of $300 million and the two organizations have total compensation for the time of $75 million, at that point, the organization with the more modest investor value is giving a more prominent profit from value since it is procuring a similar overall gain with less weight.

Increasing Earnings Per Share (EPS)

Even though a few kinds of EPS and the measure of money acquired on a for each offer premise doesn't recount the entire tale about how a business is run, an organization whose income for every offer is expanding over the long run is presumably accomplishing something right. Financial backers regularly look for organizations with an expanding EPS, yet further examination ought to be done to guarantee that the EPS numbers are the consequence of certifiable income from real transactions.

Projected Earnings

Numerous informal investors and momentary financial backers give close consideration to projected income declarations since they can have both prompt and future impacts on an organization's stock cost. Indeed, numerous financial backers bring in money exchanging income declarations.

For instance, when an organization's projected profit come in higher than anticipated, the stock cost will regularly rise rapidly and afterwards pattern down before very long. However, reliable positive projected income reports will assist the stock with ascending over the long run.

Development Investing Variables

While there is no conclusive rundown of complex measurements to manage a development strategy, a couple of elements financial backer ought to consider. An examination from Merrill Lynch, for instance, discovered that development stocks beat during times of falling loan costs. It's essential to remember that development stocks are frequently quick to get hit whenever there's any hint of a slump in the economy.

Development financial backers likewise need to painstakingly consider the administration ability of a business' leader group. Accomplishing development is among the most troublesome difficulties for a firm. In this way, a heavenly administration group is required. Financial backers should observe how the group performs and the methods by which it accomplishes development. Development is of little worth if it's completed with substantial getting. Simultaneously, financial backers ought to assess the opposition. An organization may appreciate a heavenly story, yet on the off chance that its essential item is handily reproduced, the drawn-out possibilities are faint.

GoPro is a perfect representation of this marvel. The once high-flying stock has seen regular yearly income decays since 2015. "Soon after its introduction, shares dramatically multiplied the IPO cost of $24 to as much as $87," the Wall Street Journal reported. The stock has exchanged well underneath its IPO cost. Quite a bit of this end is ascribed to the effortlessly imitated plan. GoPro is, at its centre, a little camera in a container. The rising notoriety and nature of cell phone cameras offer a modest option in contrast to paying $400 to $600 for a one-work piece of gear. In addition, the organization has been fruitless at planning and delivering new items, which is an essential advance to supporting development—something development financial backers should consider.

Makes a good growth stock

To change development putting into a manageable strategy, financial backers should figure out how to distinguish values that have the most potential to become development stocks. While the accompanying rundown isn't thorough, here are the three significant standards for spotting great development stocks:

Search for new, high-rising enterprises: The principal activity is to search for more up to date ventures and areas displaying more grounded than normal development.

"Development putting tends to live in more current enterprises where client acknowledgment is developing from an exceptionally low level, say cell phones as a chronicled model. Development stocks are distinguished by how quick their incomes and profit are developing comparative with the market," says Massocca.

It's insufficient for financial backers to distinguish development areas and put resources into any beginning phase organization they can discover. It's also imperative to get your work done on what any given organization is doing and how they fit into their industry.

Assess future income power: Another significant territory to consider is the future income Momentum of an organization, which means its capacity to produce benefits over the long haul. This should be possible by looking at its profit from resources (ROA) and its profit from value (ROE), just like its present incomes, resources, and benefits.

"While choosing development stocks, it is imperative to comprehend the plan of action of the organizationorganization, their profit power into the future," says Niladri Mukherjee.

Evaluate the nature of senior administration: obviously, it's insufficient to just gander at an organization's area and its present-day financials. If you need a smart thought of whether it truly can develop soundly into the future, you'll likewise have to think about the nature of its senior administration.

This implies seeing its board and leaders, checking their experience and history. If nobody in senior administration has any significant level of involvement, it could be unsafe to expect that the organization will perform unequivocally and reasonably.

Besides scouring new companies and developing markets, one enticement might be recognizing potential development stocks by searching for starting public contributions. Such IPOs will, in general, be held by organizations in high-development areas and may guarantee higher-than-normal returns.

Notwithstanding, research proposes that IPOs aren't just about as beneficial as many may expect, with authentic information gathered by the University of Florida's Jay Ritter showing that around 60% of IPOs have negative returns for a very long time following their openings.

Notwithstanding such risks, one more secure choice might be to put resources into a common asset or ETF, which tracks development stocks and areas, holding an assortment of organizations in its portfolio.

"An ETF gives a financially savvy approach to get openness to a list of development stocks," says Niladri Mukherjee.

Probably the most well-known development ETFs include:

- iShares Russell 1000 Growth ETF

- Invesco QQQ ETF

- Vanguard Information Technology ETF

- O'Shares Global Internet Giants ETF

For instance, the iShares Russell 1000 Growth ETF tracks around 500 of the best-performing enormous U.S. stocks. It recorded an arrival of 37.2% for the year to September 2020, contrasted with an appearance of 13% and 6.6%, separately, for the S&P 500 and the Dow Jones. The NASDAQ rose by 45.8% over a similar period, so not all high-development assets might be more productive than only putting resources into an investment that tracks a file.

In like manner, here's a little choice of the most prominent and best-performing development shared assets:

- Fidelity Trend Fund

- Zevenbergen Growth Fund

- T. Rowe Price Blue Chip Growth Fund

- Franklin DynaTech Fund

Momentum financial backers ride the wave. They accept victors continue winning, and washouts continue to lose. They hope to purchase stocks encountering an upturn. Since they take failures to keep on dropping, they may decide to short-sell those protections. In any case, short-selling is an unsafe practice. More on that later.

Consider Momentum financial backers specialized investigators. This implies they utilize a rigorously information-driven way to deal with exchanging and search at designs in stock costs to manage their buying choices. Momentum financial backers act in insubordination of the productive market speculation (EMH). This speculation expresses that resource costs completely mirror all data accessible to the general population. It's hard to accept this assertion and be a Momentum financial backer, given that the strategy looks to profit by underestimated and exaggerated values.

The Father of Momentum Investing

Even though not the primary Momentum financial backer, Richard Driehaus took the training and made it into the strategy he used to run his assets. His way of thinking was that more money could be caused by "purchasing high and selling higher" than purchasing undervalued stocks and hanging tight for the market to rethink them.

Driehaus trusted in selling the washouts and allowing the champs to ride while re-putting the money from the failures in different stocks that were starting to bubble. Large numbers of the procedures he utilized turned into the rudiments of what is currently called Momentum contributing.

Precepts of Momentum Investing

Momentum contributing looks to exploit market unpredictability by taking momentary situations in which stocks are going up and selling them when they indicate going down. The financial backer, at that point, moves the cash flow to new positions. For this situation, the market unpredictability resembles waves in the sea. A Momentum financial backer cruises up the peak of one to leap to the next wave before the primary wave crashes down once more.

A Momentum financial backer hopes to exploit financial backer crowding by standing out and being the first to take the money and run.

Elements of Momentum Investing

Exchanging Momentum markets require modern danger the board rules to address unpredictability, packing, and covered up traps that decrease benefits. Market players regularly disregard these principles; dazed by a mind-boggling dread, they'll miss the assembly or selloff while every other person books bonus benefits. The standards can be separated into five components:

- Determination, or what values you pick

- Hazard rotate around timing in opening and shutting the exchanges

- Section timing implies getting into the business early

- Position the board couples wide spreads and your holding period

- Leave focuses on requiring reliable graphing

Momentum Security Selection

Pick fluid protections while taking part in Momentum techniques. Avoid utilized or reverse ETFs because their value swings don't precisely follow basic records or fates markets because of complex asset development. Standard subsidizes make magnificent exchanging vehicles; however, they will generally crush through more modest rate gains and misfortunes contrasted and singular protections.

Search out protections that exchange over 5 million offers each day at whatever point conceivable. Numerous well-known stocks meet these rules. However, even common buoy issues can transform into exceptionally fluid instruments when news stream and extreme passionate responses attract market players from different sources.

Save watch for "today's special," when new items, divisions or ideas catch the public's creative mind, driving experts to discard computations and re-process benefit gauges. Biotechs and little to medium size innovation organizations make a liberal inventory of these story stocks.

Tight Risk Control

The dangerous side of the condition should be tended to in detail, or the Momentum strategy will come up short. The traps of Momentum exchanging include:

- I was hopping into a position too early before an Momentum move is affirmed.

- They are shutting the position past the point of no return after immersion has been reached.

- You neglect to keep your eyes on the screen, missing evolving patterns, inversions or indications of information that shock the market.

- They are keeping a position open for the time being. Stocks are especially defenceless to outside factors happening after the end of that day's exchanging – these components could cause fundamentally various costs and examples the following day.

- You neglect to act rapidly to close a terrible position, consequently riding the Momentum train the incorrect path down the tracks.

Perfect Entry Timing

The best Momentum exchanges come when a news stun hits, setting off rapid development starting with one value level then onto the next. Thus, this sets off purchasing or selling signals for discerning players who hop in and are remunerated with moment benefits. Another group of Momentum capital enters as the exchange develops, producing counter swings that shake out powerless hands. The hot money populace at long last hits a limit, setting off unpredictable whipsaws and significant inversions.

Early positions offer the best price with the least danger while maturing patterns should be kept away from no matter what. The inverse occurs in real situations because most merchants don't see the chance until late in the cycle and afterwards neglect to act until every other person hops in.

Position Management

The board set aside some effort to dominate because these protections frequently convey wide bid/ask spreads. Wide spreads require bigger development in support of yourself to arrive at productivity while likewise crushing through wide intraday ranges that uncover stops—even though technicals stay flawless.

Pick your holding period astutely because hazard expands the more you stay situated. Day exchanging functions admirably with Momentum techniques; however, it powers players to take bigger situations to make up for the more prominent benefit capability of multi-day holds. On the other hand, it is ideal for decreasing position size when holding through numerous meetings to consider more noteworthy development and prevent situation further away from the current activity.

Profitable Exits

Leave when the cost is moving quickly into an overextended specialized state. This overextended state is frequently recognized by a progression of vertical bars on the hour-long graph. Then again, the cost could penetrate the third or fourth standard deviation of a top or base 20-day Bollinger Band.

Straighten out stops or consider a visually impaired leave when technical hindrances are strike like a significant trendline or past high/low. Exit or take halfway benefits when hybrids signal potential pattern changes.

Advantages of Momentum Investing

Momentum putting can transform into huge benefits for the dealer who has the correct character, deal with the dangers implied, and devote themselves to adhering to the strategy.

Potential for High Profits Over a Short Period

There are practical benefits to be produced using Momentum contribution. For instance, say you purchase a stock that develops from $50 to $75 dependent on an excessively sure investigator report. You, at that point, sell at a benefit of the half before the stock cost revises itself. You've made a half return throughout half a month or months (not an annualized return). After some time, the benefit potential increment utilizing Momentum contributing can be incredibly huge.

Utilizing the Market's Volatility to Your Advantage

The way to Momentum contributing has the option to exploit irregular market patterns. Momentum financial backers search for stocks to put resources into that are on their way up and afterwards sell them before the costs begin to return down. For such financial backers, being in front of the pack is an approach to expand profit from investment (ROI).

Utilizing the Emotional Decisions of Other Investors

As per Ben Carlson of the blog A Wealth of Common Sense, the whole thought of Momentum contributing is worked around pursuing execution. In any case, Momentum financial backers to do this efficiently that incorporates a particular purchasing point and selling point. Maybe then be constrained by passionate reactions to stock costs like numerous financial backers. Momentum financial backers look to exploit the progressions in stock costs brought about by enthusiastic financial backers.

Disadvantages of Momentum Investing

Notwithstanding, for each silver-lined cloud, there may likewise be a downpour. Momentum contributing additionally has a few disadvantages. A similar danger return tradeoff that exists with other putting techniques additionally plays a hand in Momentum contributing.

Like a boat attempting to cruise on the peaks of waves, a Momentum financial backer is consistently in danger of timing a purchase inaccurately and winding up submerged. Most Momentum financial backers acknowledge this danger as an instalment for the chance of more significant yields.

High Turnover

High stock turnover can be costly regarding expenses. Even though minimal effort representatives are gradually stopping high charges, this is as yet a significant worry for most newbie Momentum dealers.

Time Intensive

Momentum financial backers need to screen market subtleties day by day, if not hourly. Since they manage stocks that will peak and go down once more, they need to hop in ahead of schedule and get out quick. This implies observing every one of the updates to check whether there is any regrettable news that will frighten financial backers.

Market Sensitive

Momentum putting works best in a positively trending market since financial backers will, in the general group, significantly more. In a bear market, the edge for benefit on Momentum puts contracts per expanded financial backer alert.

Does it Work?

Just like the case with so numerous other contributing styles, the appropriate response is confounded. We should investigate.

Ransack Arnott, executive and organizer of Research Affiliates, investigated this inquiry, and this is the thing that he found. "No U.S. common asset with 'Momentum' in its name has, since its initiation, beated their benchmark net of charges and expenses."

Strangely, Arnott's exploration likewise showed that recreated portfolios that put a hypothetical Momentum contributing strategy to work really "add exceptional worth, in most time-frames and in most resource classes."8 However, when utilized in a real situation, the outcomes are poor. Why? In two words: exchanging costs. The entirety of that purchasing and selling works up a ton of business and commission expenses.

Dealers who cling to an Momentum strategy should be at the switch and prepared to purchase and sell consistently. Benefits work over months, not years. This is rather than basic purchase and-hold procedures that take a set it-and-fail to remember its approach.

For the individuals who take mid-day breaks or essentially don't have a premium in watching the market each day, there are Momentum-style trade-exchangeable assets (ETFs). These offers give a financial backer admittance to a bin of stocks considered normal for Momentum protection.

The Appeal of Momentum Investing

Despite a portion of its deficiencies, Momentum contributing has its allure. Consider, for instance, that "The MSCI World Momentum Index has arrived at the midpoint of yearly gains of 7.3% in the course of recent many years, double that of the more extensive benchmark." This return most likely doesn't represent exchanging costs and the time needed for execution.

Ongoing examination discovers it very well might be feasible to effectively exchange a Momentum strategy without the requirement for full-time exchanging and research. Utilizing U.S. information from the New York Stock Exchange (NYSE) somewhere in the range of 1991 and 2010, a recent report tracked down that an improved on Momentum strategy beat the benchmark even after representing exchange costs. Also, a base investment of $5,000 was sufficient to understand the benefits.9

A similar exploration found that contrasting this essential strategy with one of the more constant, more modest exchanges showed the last beat it, yet just to a certain extent. At some point or another, the exchanging expenses of a quickfire approach disintegrated the profits. Even better, the scientists discovered that "the ideal Momentum exchanging recurrence goes from bi-yearly to month to month"— a shockingly sensible pace.

Shorting

As referenced before, Momentumful Momentum brokers may utilize short selling to support their profits. This procedure permits a financial backer to benefit from a drop in a resource's cost. For instance, the quick vendor—accepting security will fall in price—gets 50 offers, adding up to $100. Then, the short merchant quickly sells those offers on the market for $100 and afterwards trusts that the resource will drop. At the point when it does, they repurchase the 50 offers (so they can be gotten back to the moneylender) at, suppose, $25.

Subsequently, the short merchant acquired $100 on the underlying deal, at that point, burned through $25 to get the offers back for an addition of $75.

The issue with this strategy is that there is a limitless drawback hazard. In ordinary contributing, the drawback hazard is the absolute worth of your investment. On the off chance that you donate $100, the most you can lose is $100. In any case, with short selling, your greatest conceivable misfortune is boundless. In the situation above, for instance, you acquire 50 offers and sell them for $100. In any case, maybe the stock doesn't drop true to form. It goes up.

The 50 offers are valued at $150, at that point $200, etc. Eventually, the short merchant should repurchase the offers to return them to the bank. On the off chance that the offer cost continues to build, this will be a costly recommendation.

Strategy 4: Dollar-Cost Averaging

Dollar-cost averaging (DCA) is the act of making ordinary investments in the market over the long run and isn't fundamentally unrelated to different strategies depicted previously. Maybe, it is a method for executing whatever process you picked. With DCA, you may decide to put $300 in an investment account each month. This restrained methodology turns out to be especially amazing when you utilize mechanized highlights that contribute to you. It's not difficult to focus on an arrangement when the interaction requires no oversight.

The advantage of the DCA strategy is that it maintains a strategic distance from the agonizing and disastrous strategy of market timing. Indeed, even prepared financial backers sporadically feel the compulsion to purchase when they think costs are low to find. Regrettably, they have a more drawn out approach to drop.

When investments occur in standard additions, the financial backer catches costs at all levels, from high to low. These intermittent investments viably below the normal per share cost of the buys. Giving DCA something to do implies settling on three boundaries:

- The all-out whole to be contributed

- The window of time during which the investments will be made

- The recurrence of buys

A Wise Choice

Dollar-cost averaging is an intelligent decision for most financial backers. It keeps you focused on saving while at the same time lessening the degree of hazard and the impacts of unpredictability. However, for those in the situation to contribute a precise amount, DCA may not be the best methodology.

"By and large, we track down that a LSI (singular amount investment) approach has outflanked a DCA approach roughly 66% of the time, in any event, when results are adapted to the higher instability of a stock/bond portfolio versus cash investments."

However, most financial backers are not in a situation to make a solitary, enormous investment. Like this, DCA is proper for most. Besides, a DCA approach is a successful countermeasure to the intellectual predisposition innate to people. New and experienced financial backers the same are powerless to hard-wired imperfections in judgment. Misfortune repugnance predisposition, for instance, makes us see the increase or loss of a measure of money lopsidedly. Furthermore, affirmation inclination drives us to zero in on and recall data that affirms our since a long time ago held convictions while disregarding opposing data that might be significant.

Dollar-cost averaging goes around these normal issues by eliminating human frailties from the condition. Customary, mechanized investments forestall unconstrained, nonsensical conduct. A similar Vanguard study finished up, "If the financial backer is essentially worried about limiting disadvantage hazard and expected sensations of disappointment (coming about because of singular amount contributing preceding a market decline), at that point DCA might be of use."10

Once you've Identified Your Strategy

So you've limited a strategy. Fantastic! Be that as it may, there are as yet a couple of things you'll have to do before you put aside the initial instalment into your investment account.

To begin with, sort out how much money you need to cover your investments. That incorporates the amount you can store from the outset and the amount you can keep on contributing going ahead.

You'll, at that point, need to choose the ideal path for you to contribute. Do you plan to go to a conventional financial consultant or representative, or is an inactive, straightforward methodology more fitting for you? On the off chance that you pick the last mentioned, consider joining with a Robo consultant. This will help you sort out the cost of contributing from the board expenses to commissions you'll have to pay your dealer or counsellor. Something else to remember: Don't dismiss manager supported 401ks — that is an extraordinary method to begin contributing. Most organizations permit you to contribute part of your check and hide it tax-exempt, and many will coordinate with your commitments. You will not receive notification since you don't need to do a thing.

Think about your investment vehicles. Recollect that it doesn't assist with keeping your eggs in a single bin, so make sure you spread your money around to various investment vehicles by broadening—stocks, bonds, common assets, ETFs. In case you're socially conscious, you may think about capable of contributing. This is the ideal opportunity to sort out what you need your investment portfolio to be made of and what it will resemble.

Constructing a portfolio can likewise raise such intricacies as to how best to adjust the danger of certain investments against their expected returns. Consider finding support. Given innovation and the furious rivalry for your investments, more assets than any time in recent memory are accessible. Those alternatives incorporate Robo-consultants, remote helpers that can assist you with making a reasonable portfolio at a low cost, and charge just financial counsellors, who don't rely upon pay from commissions on the items they sell you. Put your exchanging abilities under serious scrutiny with our FREE Stock Simulator. Rival a great many Investopedia merchants and exchange your way to the top! Submit exchanges a virtual climate before you begin taking a chance with your own money. Work on exchanging systems so when you're prepared to enter the open market, you've had the training you need. The hardest piece of contributing is beginning, yet the sooner you do, the more you should make. That's all there is to it. Contributing can get muddled; however, the essentials are basic. Amplify the sum you save and your manager's commitments. Limit assessments and expenses. Settle on brilliant decisions with your restricted assets.

Constructing a portfolio can likewise raise such intricacies as to how best to adjust the danger of certain investments against their expected returns. Consider finding support. Given innovation and the furious rivalry for your investments, more assets than any time in recent memory are accessible. Those choices incorporate Robo-counselors, remote helpers that can assist you with making a decent portfolio at a low cost, and expense just financial consultants, who don't rely upon pay from commissions on the items they sell you. Put your exchanging abilities under a magnifying glass with our FREE Stock Simulator. Contend with a large number of Investopedia brokers and exchange your way to the top! Submit exchanges a virtual climate before you begin taking a chance with your own money. Work on exchanging techniques so when you're prepared to enter the open market, you've had the training you need. The hardest piece of contributing is beginning; however, the sooner you do, the more you should make. That's all there is to it.

Contributing is an exciting ride, so keep your feelings under control. It might appear to be stunning when your investments are bringing in money, yet it could be hard to deal with when they assume a misfortune. That is the reason it's essential to make a stride back, remove your feelings from the condition and audit your investments with your guide consistently to ensure they're on target.

Get started investing as early as possible

Contributing when you're youthful is perhaps the most ideal approaches to see strong profits from your money. That is on account of compound profit, which implies your investment returns begin procuring their return. Compounding permits your record equilibrium to accelerate after some time.

How that functions, by and by: Let's say you contribute $200 consistently for a very long time and acquire a 6% normal yearly return. Toward the finish of the 10-year time frame, you'll have $33,300. Of that sum, $24,200 is money you've contributed — that $ 200 month to month commitments — and $9,100 is revenue you've procured on your investment.

There will be high points and low points in the stock market, obviously, however contributing youthful methods, you have a long time to brave them — and a very long time for your money to develop. Start now, regardless of whether you need to begin little.

If you're as yet unconvinced by the force of contributing, utilize our expansion adding machine to perceive how swelling can cut into your reserve funds if you don't contribute.

Decide how much to invest

The amount you ought to contribute relies upon your investment objective and when you need to arrive at it.

One common investment objective is retirement. On the off chance that you have a retirement account at work, similar to a 401(k), and it offers to coordinate with dollars, your first contributing achievement is simple: Contribute at any rate enough to that record to acquire the full match. That is free money, and you would prefer not to pass it up.

When in doubt of thumb, you need to mean to contribute an aggregate of 10% to 15% of your pay every year for retirement — your manager match checks toward that objective. That may sound ridiculous now; however, you can move gradually dependent upon it after some time.

For other contributing objectives, think about your time skyline and the sum you need; at that point, work in reverse to separate that sum into the month-to-month or week after week investments.

Open an investment account

If you don't have a 401(k), you can put for retirement in an individual retirement account, similar to a conventional or Roth IRA.

If you're contributing for another objective, you probably need to keep away from retirement accounts — which are intended to be utilized for retirement and subsequently have limitations about when and how you can take your money back out — and pick an available investment fund. You can eliminate money from a general investment fund whenever.

A typical misinterpretation is that you need a ton of money to open an investment account or begin contributing. That is just false. (We even have a guide for how to contribute $500.) Many online specialists, which offer the two IRAs and standard financier investment accounts, require no base investment to open a record. There are many assets accessible for moderately limited quantities.

Regardless of whether you contribute through a 401(k) or comparable boss supported retirement plan, in a customary or Roth IRA, or a standard investment account, you pick what to put resources into.

It's essential to see each instrument and how much danger it conveys. The most famous investments for those simply beginning include:

Stocks

A stock is a portion of proprietorship in a solitary organization. Stocks are otherwise called values.

Stocks are bought at an offer cost, going from the single digits a few thousand dollars, contingent upon the organization. We suggest buying stocks through shared assets, which we'll detail underneath.

Bonds

A bond is a credit to an organization or government element, which consents to take care of you in a specific number of years. Meanwhile, you get interested.

Bonds by and large are safer than stocks since you know precisely when you'll be repaid and the amount you'll procure. Be that as it may, bonds acquire lower long haul returns, so they should make up just a little piece of a drawn-out investment portfolio.

Mutual funds

A common asset is a combination of investments bundled as one. Common assets permit financial backers to skirt crafted by picking singular stocks and bonds and rather buy a different assortment in one exchange. The innate expansion of shared assets makes them, by and large, safer than distinct stocks.

An expert oversees some common assets, yet file reserves — a kind of shared asset — follow the presentation of a particular stock market file, similar to the S&P 500. By disposing of the expert administration, list reserves can charge lower expenses than effectively oversaw shared assets.

Most 401(k)s offer a curated determination of shared or record assets with no base investment, yet outside of those plans, these assets may require at least $1,000 or more.

Chapter 3: Day Trading Psychology

Psychology trading reflects the attitudes and mind state which helps in the determination of securities trading in the success or the failure. This psychology of trading reflects various facets of the behaviors and character of someone which affect their trading activities. Trading psychology can be as important in trading performance assessments as qualities like expertise, ability, and experience. Risk-taking and discipline are the most two important facets of the psychology of trading since such elements execution by an investor are crucial to the performance of the trading strategy. While greed and fear are the common two most known emotions related to trading psychology, hope and regret are emotions that control the behavior of trading.

Key Takeaways

- Trading psychology is the emotional dimension of investor decision-making processes and can help to understand why certain decisions appear more logical than other decisions.
- The trading psychology is characterized primarily by the influence of greed and fear.
- Greed influences decisions which seem too risky to accept.
- Fear drives choices in life that seem risk-free and produce too little return.

7.1 Understanding Trading Psychology

Investing psychology might be related to some different feelings and actions that are also catalysts for investing in markets. Standard characterizations of motivated conduct emotionally in markets ascribe either fear or greed to certain emotional trading. Greed is an extreme appetite for money that can be described, so intense that it affects often judgment and reason.

So, greed inspired trade or investor definition suggests the feeling sometimes drives traders through a range of behaviors.

It may involve making risky investments, purchasing business untested or product stock only due to increasingly growing in size, or purchasing securities without the investment underlying investigating. In fact, greed can encourage investors to remain longer in lucrative trades than is prudent in an attempt to squeeze out extra income from it or to take up big speculative positions. Greed is more apparent in the final period of bull markets, where optimism becomes rife and the wind becomes granted caution by the buyers.

Conversely, fear causes traders to prematurely close down positions or refrain from risk-taking due to concerns about large losses. In bear markets, panic is tangible, and it's a strong emotion that can lead traders and buyers to behave irrationally in their rush to escape. Fear also morphs into hysteria, which usually allows the hysteria sale to trigger major sealing in the market. Regret will lead a trader to resume a trade after originally overlooking it because the product was going too quickly. That is a market rule breach, which also contributes to significant losses from protection rates dropping from peak highs.

7.2 Technical Analysis

Psychology trading is also essential for analysts to push their decisions of trading by depending on the techniques of charting. Security charting may offer a perspective broad variety on the progress of a system. Although charting and technical analysis strategies can be helpful in spotting trends for selling and buying opportunities, movements of the market require awareness and insight, which is extracted from the psychology of trading of an individual. During charting, several occasions are there where an investor will focus not just on the chart experience but also on protection understanding observed by them and the intuition about how larger variables influence the sector.

Traders with a keen focus on market factors that are comprehensive for discipline, security, and confidence display trading psychology that is balanced which usually contributes to profitable performance.

7.3 DAY TRADING TERMINOLOGIES

The field of day-trading have terminologies like every technological business. Although these terminologies seem completely common to seasoned traders, it may mislead new traders. Learning jargon shouldn't be the toughest trading part, just be sure you learn these specific words and acronyms. In day trading 35 specific terminologies are used:-

1- week 52 high/low – A stock when hits a highest or lowest of the year

2- After Hrs. – Trading is conducted after the closure of the market

3- Ask – The willing price of the seller. (The ask price lowest is referenced commonly)

4- Bid – The willing price of the buyer. (The bid price highest is referenced commonly)

5- Breakouts – "breaks out" of stock above the level of resistance previously.

6- Candlesticks – A chart type that represents each candle, low, high, close & open for a period given.

'

7- Covering – Sold short shares buying back.

8- ETF (Exchange-traded Fund)– consists of equities set.

9- E/R (Earnings Reports) – A company's financials report quarterly/annual.

10- Filing – A SEC, filed document with regarding updates of the company.

11- Float – For public trading the available shares amount.

12- F/A (Fundamental Analysis) – A company analysis along with its industry (filings, sector, financials, etc.)

13- Up/Down Gap – Above or below to the closing price previously when opens the stock.

14- Going Long – stock buying with the plan of later higher price selling.

15- HOD/LOD High/Low of the Day– A stock's day price, highest or lowest.

16- Hard borrowing stock – A stock not available readily to short. An additional fee might be charged by the Brokers to those who wanted to short the hard stock to borrow.

17- Liquidity – A stock that can be easily bought or sold and is not affecting the price of the stock's drastically.

18- Low Float –Traded shares publicly stock's in less amount, often higher volatility times experiencing.

19- Market makers – The companies responsible for the facilitation of orders of buying& selling and in the markets liquidity maintenance.

ì

20- Market Cap – A company dollar total value based on outstanding shares and stock price.

21- Outstanding Shares – issued shares number consisting of both the institutional and float ownership

22- Pre-Market – before the opening of the market, trading is done.

23- P&L (Profits & Losses)– For a period given, gains/losses of a portfolio.

24- PDT Rule for Pattern Day Trader– A limiting traders SEC rule with under 25,000 dollars in accounts to a 4-day trades in 5 days maximum.

25- PR – A press release issued by a company

26- From Green to Red and From Red To Green – A stock when goes from up to down on a day or from bottom to up.

27- R (Resistance) – A level of price at which repeatedly sellers overpower the buyers, and making for the stock difficult in the price increases.

28- Risk/Reward – Money that on the trade you can risk in comparison to the expectation of profit.

29- Scalp – Very little changes in price and advantages taken with this.

30- Short Selling – a stock shares selling that are not owned by you in the hopes of lower price shares buying (going long opposite)

31- Spread – The difference in price between the ask and the bid.

32- Support – A level of price at which repeatedly buyers overwhelm sellers to make for the stock difficult to lower drop in the price.

33- TA (Technical Analysis) – The historical price of stock's action analysis (by the use of technical indicators and charts) for future movement prediction.

34- Trend – The movement of the price of stock's in the direction generally. In a trend up or down stock might be.

35- Volume – For a time given, the shares amount of stock trades.

FAQ's About Day Trading

Is Day Trading Part-Time?

Yeah, but stay on watch. Intraday roles should never be left unattended. You don't want to put before work a trade for starters, and then see what's going on. When you're looking to sell part-time, the plan is tailored for your timetable. You might choose to swap open market or close market, or you may choose to keep for several days the positions at a time.

Expected Revenue Generation Day Trader Can Make?

"How much money will a dealer earn in a day?

"When it comes to day trading, certainly a wide variety of profit opportunities.

Some citizens will also choose to work another career, however they tend to make some income out of it. Single month, from business by day trading. There are those that can happily survive with what they're doing day trading and there's the tiny amount that's going to raise a ton. There's still a big community of want-to-be traders who are going to struggle and never earn profits.

How Can One Judge The Right Broker?

Every broker has their own pros and cons. Defines what you expect from a broker, and determines the right match broker.

For example, if transaction fees are everything you think about, then choose the broker with the lowest commissions. If you base your strategy on short selling, choose a broker with better short lists.

What Are Different Categories of Brokers?

In three categories falls the difference mainly

1. Fees – Routing, platform account fees, commissions etc.

2. Tools –mobile& trading platforms, tools for research, etc.

3. Features –leverage, shortlists, services located, etc.

Repeat – It is an endless operation, for traders also that are experienced. Of course, when you're able, the "Check" stage will gradually move from trading of paper to trading in real.

How Much Is Expected To Make By Day Trading?

A strange query is this – as though there were a response that might mean that trading isn't the time worth of yours.

You can ask the question firstly that, "May I transact money? "Most traders crash, and you've outperformed traders mostly by reaching some degree of consistent productivity.

On the dealer, the plan, and the scale of the portfolio It depends, as to how much you will raise. No definite response has been given.

What Basic Tools Are Required For Day Trading?

An Internet link, a stock trader, and data some type (i.e. news, maps, level two, etc.) would be required. The appropriate data differs by trader. Traders mostly need a data real-time trading network. When you use them, you should attach resources to the toolkit-no waiting need for some device until you use it.

What Day Trading Risks Are?

Day trading is just as it looks like: purchasing and selling within a day — trading — a stock, or a number of stocks. It is all about forecasting and managing the demand, with the goal of making a small return on rising exchange. Those little gains, in a perfect future, add up to a major gain. Yet analysis has found that just 1 per cent of day traders gain money consistently; others, others lose it. It's essentially a full-time job, because you need to be continuously monitoring the market — and timing — waiting for the next step.

It's not for companies starting out, or casual. If you are interested in day trading, our recommendation is to allocate to the strategy a small portion of your overall portfolio – no more than 5% or 10%, tops. This means, if you lose money — at least at first, because you are sure to do — such losses should be at least limited. The rest of the assets will be long-term savings.

Day Trading Is Not Illegal

Trading by day is not unlawful. The Securities and Exchange Commission does, though, enforce strict rules on trend day traders. The SEC describes day trading as purchasing and selling or short-selling on the same day, often purchasing the same security — often a portfolio. Under SEC a model day trader:

Four times or more Day-trades within five days of business Such day trades account for more than 6% of their overall trading volume across the five-day period. You are expected to have at least $25,000 in equity in your account if you fall into that group. That holding may be in cash or in securities.

Conclusion

Putting away money may appear to be threatening, particularly on the off chance that you've never done it. In any case, if you sort out how you need to contribute, how much money you ought to contribute, and your danger resistance, you'll be all around situated to make savvy choices with your money that will work well for you for quite a long time to come. As should be obvious, a few kinds of investment systems take into account pretty much every degree of hazard, inclusion, and timing. Tracking down the best strategy for you will boil down to understanding your inclinations and financial circumstance. The best thing I can prescribe is to do your examination — what turns out incredible for a companion may not work for you. There is a great deal influencing everything regarding contributing, however with the correct assurance, you can discover a strategy that supports your financial wellbeing and assists you with accomplishing your objectives. Your investment strategy relies upon your saving objectives, how much money you need to contact them and your time skyline.

On the off chance that your reserve funds objective is over 20 years away (like retirement), practically the entirety of your money can be in stocks. Be that as it may, picking explicit stocks can be muddled and tedious, so for the vast majority, the ideal approach to put resources into stocks is through minimal effort stock common assets, record assets or ETFs.

Suppose you're putting something aside for a short objective, and you need the money inside five years. In that case, the danger related to stocks implies you're in an ideal situation protecting your money, in an online investment account, cash the executive's record or okay investment portfolio. We layout the perfect choices for transient reserve funds here.

If you can't or don't have any desire to conclude, you can open an investment account (counting an IRA) through a robo-counsellor, an investment the executive's administration utilizes PC calculations to fabricate and take care of your investment portfolio.

Robo-counsels generally assemble their portfolios out of minimal effort ETFs and list reserves. Since they offer low costs and low or no essentials, robos let you begin rapidly. They charge a little expense for a portfolio on the board, by and large, around 0.25% of your record balance. Contributing can get muddled, yet the essentials are straightforward. Amplify the sum you save and your manager's commitments. Limit assessments and charges. Settle on wise decisions with your restricted assets.

Lightning Source UK Ltd.
Milton Keynes UK
UKHW021853270521
384511UK00002B/292